YOUR BODY
How It Works

The Immune System

YOUR BODY How It Works

YOUR BODY
How It Works

The Immune System

Gregory Stewart

Introduction by
Denton A. Cooley, M.D.
President and Surgeon-in-Chief
of the Texas Heart Institute
Clinical Professor of Surgery at the
University of Texas Medical School, Houston, Texas

CHELSEA HOUSE
P U B L I S H E R S
A Haights Cross Communications ✛ Company

Philadelphia

CHELSEA HOUSE PUBLISHERS

VP, NEW PRODUCT DEVELOPMENT Sally Cheney
DIRECTOR OF PRODUCTION Kim Shinners
CREATIVE MANAGER Takeshi Takahashi
MANUFACTURING MANAGER Diann Grasse

Staff for THE IMMUNE SYSTEM

EDITOR Beth Reger
PRODUCTION ASSISTANT Megan Emery
PHOTO EDITOR Sarah Bloom
SERIES & COVER DESIGNER Terry Mallon
LAYOUT 21st Century Publishing and Communications, Inc.

A Haights Cross Communications◆Company

www.chelseahouse.com

First Printing

1 3 5 7 9 8 6 4 2

Library of Congress Cataloging-in-Publication Data

Stewart, Gregory, 1957-
  The immune system / by Gregory Stewart.
    p. cm. -- (Your body: how it works)
  Includes index.
  Contents: How important is the immune system? -- Innate immunity and
defenses -- The organs, tissues, and cells of the immune system -- The humoral
immune response -- Making antibodies -- Cell-mediated immunity
-- The importance of vaccines -- Allergies and autoimmune diseases -- Immunity
as a tool for scientists.
  ISBN 0-7910-7630-X
  1. Immune system--Juvenile literature. [1. Immune system.] I. Title. II. Series.
QR181.8.S74 2003
616.07'9--dc21
                                                                2003013669

Table of Contents

Introduction

The human body is an incredibly complex and amazing structure. At best, it is a source of strength, beauty, and wonder. We can compare the healthy body to a well-designed machine whose parts work smoothly together. We can also compare it to a symphony orchestra in which each instrument has a different part to play. When all of the musicians play together, they produce beautiful music.

From a purely physical standpoint, our bodies are made mainly of water. We are also made of many minerals, including calcium, phosphorous, potassium, sulfur, sodium, chlorine, magnesium, and iron. In order of size, the elements of the body are organized into cells, tissues, and organs. Related organs are combined into systems, including the musculoskeletal, cardio-vascular, nervous, respiratory, gastrointestinal, endocrine, and reproductive systems.

Our cells and tissues are constantly wearing out and being replaced without our even knowing it. In fact, much of the time, we take the body for granted. When it is working properly, we tend to ignore it. Although the heart beats about 100,000 times per day and we breathe more than 10 million times per year, we do not normally think about these things. When something goes wrong, however ,our bodies tell us through pain and other symptoms. In fact, pain is a very effective alarm system that lets us know the body needs attention. If the pain does not go away, we may need to see a doctor. Even without medical help, the body has an amazing ability to heal itself. If we cut ourselves, the blood clotting system works to seal the cut right away, and the immune defense system sends out special blood cells that are programmed to heal the area.

During the past 50 years, doctors have gained the ability to repair or replace almost every part of the body. In my own field of cardiovascular surgery, we are able to open the heart and repair its valves, arteries, chambers, and connections. In many cases, these repairs can be done through a tiny "keyhole" incision that speeds up patient recovery and leaves hardly any scar. If the entire heart is diseased, we can replace it altogether, either with a donor heart or with a mechanical device. In the future, the use of mechanical hearts will probably be common in patients who would otherwise die of heart disease.

Until the mid-twentieth century, infections and contagious diseases related to viruses and bacteria were the most common causes of death. Even a simple scratch could become infected and lead to death from "blood poisoning." After penicillin and other antibiotics became available in the 1930s and 40s, doctors were able to treat blood poisoning, tuberculosis, pneumonia, and many other bacterial diseases. Also, the introduction of modern vaccines allowed us to prevent childhood illnesses, smallpox, polio, flu, and other contagions that used to kill or cripple thousands.

Today, plagues such as the "Spanish flu" epidemic of 1918–19 , which killed 20 to 40 million people worldwide, are unknown except in history books. Now that these diseases can be avoided, people are living long enough to have long-term (chronic) conditions such as cancer, heart failure, diabetes, and arthritis. Because chronic diseases tend to involve many organ systems or even the whole body, they cannot always be cured with surgery. These days, researchers are doing a lot of work at the cellular level, trying to find the underlying causes of chronic illnesses. Scientists recently finished mapping the human genome, which is a set of coded "instructions" programmed into our cells. Each cell contains 3 billion "letters" of this code. By showing how the body is made, the human genome will help researchers prevent and treat disease at its source, within the cells themselves.

The body's long-term health depends on many factors, called risk factors. Some risk factors, including our age, sex, and family history of certain diseases, are beyond our control. Other important risk factors include our lifestyle, behavior, and environment. Our modern lifestyle offers many advantages but is not always good for our bodies. In western Europe and the United States, we tend to be stressed, overweight, and out of shape. Many of us have unhealthy habits such as smoking cigarettes, abusing alcohol, or using drugs. Our air, water, and food often contain hazardous chemicals and industrial waste products. Fortunately, we can do something about most of these risk factors. At any age, the most important things we can do for our bodies are to eat right, exercise regularly, get enough sleep, and refuse to smoke, overuse alcohol, or use addictive drugs. We can also help clean up our environment. These simple steps will lower our chances of getting cancer, heart disease, or other serious disorders.

These days, thanks to the Internet and other forms of media coverage, people are more aware of health-related matters. The average person knows more about the human body than ever before. Patients want to understand their medical conditions and treatment options. They want to play a more active role, along with their doctors, in making medical decisions and in taking care of their own health.

I encourage you to learn as much as you can about your body and to treat your body well. These things may not seem too important to you now, while you are young, but the habits and behaviors that you practice today will affect your physical well-being for the rest of your life. The present book series, YOUR BODY: HOW IT WORKS, is an excellent introduction to human biology and anatomy. I hope that it will awaken within you a lifelong interest in these subjects.

Denton A. Cooley, M.D.
President and Surgeon-in-Chief
of the Texas Heart Institute
Clinical Professor of Surgery at the
University of Texas Medical School, Houston, Texas

1

How Important is the Immune System?

INTRODUCTION

Many of the other systems of the human body are probably somewhat familiar to you. The skeletal system includes the bones of the body and serves as a support system for the rest of the body systems. The muscular system allows the body to move, and the digestive system allows us to take in food and convert it to forms needed to build and maintain the body. It is relatively easy to understand the functions and the importance of these systems, but what about the immune system? The immune system is extremely important to us. It is the most important system in the body for avoiding and fighting infections. It also prevents the development of certain types of cancer. To help you understand the importance of this system, we will consider two examples of conditions where the immune system does not function properly. When we understand how problems with the immune system result in these conditions, we will have a better appreciation of why an effective immune system is so important to our health and well-being.

CONDITION ONE—WHEN THE IMMUNE SYSTEM UNDER-FUNCTIONS: ACQUIRED IMMUNE DEFICIENCY SYNDROME (AIDS)

Plagues and History?

Every historical age of human history seems to be defined by one or more catastrophic diseases. In medieval Europe, "the black plague," or bubonic plague, was a recurring disease. Outbreaks would occur in villages and cities throughout Europe and in many cases were responsible for the death of up to 25% of the total population. The history of sub-Saharan Africa is marked with cycles of malaria, a disease transmitted by mosquitoes. During the exploration and colonization period of Europe, travel to far-away places brought back to the home countries very exotic products: fruits, silks, and spices, but also previously unknown diseases such as syphilis. Tuberculosis was the principal plague of the romantic and Victorian periods in England's history. This wasting disease was so prevalent that it became a central and recurring theme in much of the literature of the time. When you hear of a character suffering from, or dying of, "consumption," the author is referring to tuberculosis. Not surprisingly, human history prior to the modern age is punctuated with references to these and other devastating human diseases.

We are able to find examples of diseases that altered events in the history of the Western Hemisphere. Native American populations were free of many of the traditional European diseases, and, as a result, these populations were extremely sensitive to exposure to those diseases. Franco Pizzaro and the conquistadors who conquered and colonized much of Central and South America were known to give "gifts" to the native populations. In many cases these gifts were laden with the virus that causes smallpox, and many historians attribute the fall of the Incan Empire, one of the most advanced and sophisticated societies of human history, to the devastating effects of this early form of biological warfare. Similar strategies were used to weaken the Native American populations of North America, allowing the settlers from Europe to easily capture the lands of the Native American tribes. At the turn of the twentieth century, it was common for parents to have large families, six or more children, largely due to the fact that at least one in four of those children would die from diseases such as influenza, measles, and scarlet fever. During the 1920s and through the 1940s, the United States was devastated by polio, a disease that killed many and left many of its other victims partially para- lyzed. There is no doubt that the twentieth century was marked by a number of important diseases.

The Plague of the Modern Age—AIDS.

If there is a plague of our modern age, it is probably **Acquired Immune Deficiency Syndrome**, or AIDS. While this condition will be discussed in detail later in this volume, we will discuss the disease in brief terms here, focusing on its history and its interaction with the immune system.

AIDS is a global epidemic (Figure 1.1). We are somewhat aware of its significance within the United States, but there are areas of the world where AIDS is a much more serious epidemic. In certain villages in southern Africa, as much as 95% of the adult population is HIV positive (HIV+). HIV, or the **Human Immunodeficiency Virus**, is the causative agent for AIDS. Globally, millions of people are victims of this disease. It is a slow, progressive disease that is first indicated by rather mild symptoms that are easily confused with a cold or the flu. As the disease progresses, the symptoms become much worse, the patient will be chronically (continu- ally or repeatedly) ill, and begins to lose weight. In Africa, the continent thought to be where this disease originated, the general deterioration of health, coupled with the rapid loss of weight, has given rise to the nickname, "the wasting disease," for the progressive deterioration of health associated with cases of AIDS.

Contrary to what some people believe, AIDS is a disease that should concern us all. It is not a "gay" disease, or a "drug user" disease, although the disease in the United States first appeared in these populations. HIV does not discriminate. It is a disease of men and women, gay persons and heterosexuals, athletes and addicts. The history of AIDS in the United States is an interesting one. The highlights of this history follow.

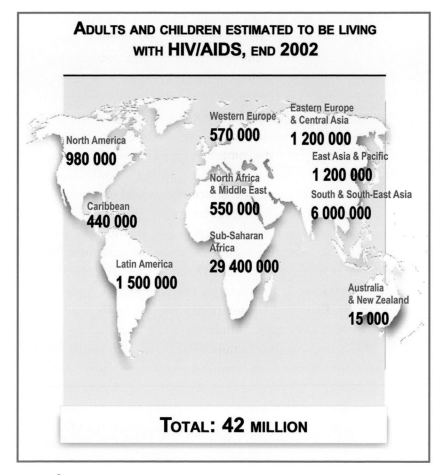

Figure 1.1 HIV/AIDS is a growing threat. Data provided by the World Health Organization (WHO) on the global distribution of HIV/AIDS (shown here) indicates that the disease is now distributed around the world, with particularly heavy distribution in Sub-Saharan Africa, Eastern Europe and Asia, and the Americas. The disease can be passed through sexual intercourse (both heterosexual and homosexual) and the transfer of blood and other bodily fluids.

The History of AIDS in the United States

To fully appreciate why and how the United States reacted to the first cases of Acquired Immune Deficiency Syndrome, it is important to consider the success we made against infectious disease in the two to three decades that preceded the AIDS epidemic. During the 1960s and 1970s, great advances were made in the area of medicine, particularly in infectious disease. Smallpox, once one of the most feared diseases in the world, had been completely eliminated. The United States was well on its way to eradicating another devastating disease, tuberculosis. We were successfully managing so many diseases with vaccines and antibiotics that some of the leading scientists of the time were suggesting that medical microbiology would soon become an extinct area of study. Colleges and universities that trained microbiologists began to reduce the emphasis on disease and increase the emphasis on biochemistry, molecular genetics, and environmental microbiology. As had happened so often in human history, we became overconfident in our success. Not surprisingly, in 1981, when new cases of unexplained infections began to occur, we were unprepared to deal with this new crisis.

The history of AIDS in the United States built slowly. In June of 1981 a report appeared in a weekly paper published by the Centers for Disease Control and Prevention (CDC). This weekly report is known as the MMWR, or *Morbidity and Mortality Weekly Report.* It is the most important tool for communicating information about diseases, illnesses, and accidents that affect human health. This particular issue reported that five young men from Los Angeles were treated at three different hospitals in the Los Angeles area for a type of pneumonia called *Pneumocystis carinii* pneumonia (PCP). These men appeared to be in good health which was unexpected as this form of pneumonia is usually only seen in people who are so ill that their immune systems are not functioning properly. The men did not know each other and the only common characteristic among them was that they were gay. Laboratory blood work indicated all five men had an unusually low level of a white blood cell called a T-helper lymphocyte, or a T_H-cell. As you will learn in later chapters

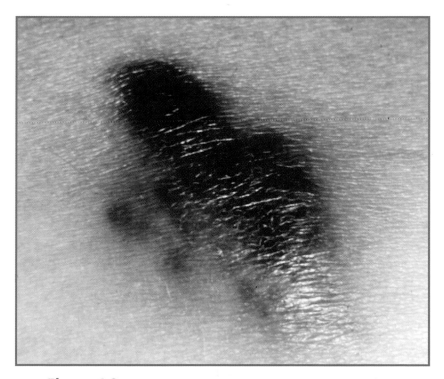

Figure 1.2 Kaposi's sarcoma, a form of cancer of the lining of the blood vessels, is associated with HIV/AIDS. As tumors develop in the lining of the blood vessels, the vessels leak blood into the tissues, resulting in the dark patches seen here. While usually seen associated with the skin, these local hemorrhages occur throughout the body.

of this book, the T-helper cell is essential for activating the immune response. With such low levels of these cells in the blood of these five men, their bodies could not fight the *Pneumocystis carinii* microbes in their lungs, resulting in fluid accumulation in the lung tissue, or pneumonia.

One month later, in July of 1981, the MMWR reported 26 cases of Kaposi's sarcoma (Figure 1.2). This is a cancer of the lining of the blood vessels. As the tumors grow, the walls of the blood vessels weaken and blood leaks into the surrounding tissues, causing reddish-purple patches that are visible under the skin. All 26 cases were young men, 20 living in New York and six living in California. Again, all of these men were gay and until recently had been in good health. Prior to this outbreak, Kaposi's sarcoma was only known to occur in older men of Mediterranean descent. Of these 26 patients, ten also had PCP, and several others had diseases usually only seen in persons who are severely immunocompromised (having immune systems that do not function properly). A number of explanations were given for these unusual cases in young gay men; however, some believe that the government was slow to respond to these diseases because all the patients diagnosed with these cases were gay. Later in 1981, the CDC reported cases of PCP in heroin addicts and other IV drug users. By early the next year, the first case of transmission between heterosexuals was reported. Late in 1982, immune deficiency began to appear in hemophiliacs and other persons who received blood transfusions. The public health community became concerned. This was no longer a "gay" disease. It was appearing in the broader population, and it appeared that even the United States blood supply might be contaminated with the unknown agent that was destroying the immune system of more and more Americans.

Cases of the disease, now known as Acquired Immune Deficiency Syndrome (AIDS), began to increase very rapidly in the United States. Shortly thereafter cases began to appear in other countries as well. A test had been developed to detect the virus that caused the disease, but there was still no cure. Some of the patients first diagnosed began to get progressively sicker and, after months of suffering, died. The World Health Organization (WHO), a branch of the United Nations, was charted by the United Nations to address global health issues. It began to hold annual meetings to monitor and report on the disease. At the Tenth International Conference on AIDS, held in 1994, some staggering statistics were revealed. It was estimated that worldwide there might be as many as 14 million persons infected with the Human Immunodeficiency Virus (HIV) that causes AIDS. In some villages in Africa, nearly 95% of the adult population, both men and women, were suspected of being HIV+. Infected women were transmitting the virus to their unborn children at alarming rates. When the infected children were born, they were weak and sick. Most died by age two. We now believe that as many as 40 million people have the disease and that it will continue to be a major health problem for at least 100 more years.

There are still many unanswered questions about the disease. We do not know how the virus found its way into the human population, nor do we know its original host. We know, however, that the disease was probably in the United States before 1981. Tissue samples that had been frozen from autopsies of persons who died of unusual pneumonias were thawed and tested with the diagnostic kit for HIV. They were positive. The susceptible populations have also changed. In the early 1980s the majority of cases were in men, particularly gay men, in IV drug users, and in both male and female prostitutes. Now researchers find the rates of new cases growing most rapidly in the heterosexual female population. The disease is known to be transmitted by sexual activity and by the transfer of blood and other bodily fluids. It is not transmitted by breathing or casual contact. HIV attacks the T-helper cells that are essential to our ability to raise an immune response. Without these cells we cannot fight infection or control certain rare forms of cancer.

The devastating disease, AIDS, has shown us just how important our immune system is. Without it, we are easy prey to disease-causing microorganisms and our own body's cells that mutate and become carcinogenic (cancer-causing). We are making progress in fighting AIDS. New drug therapies and other medical treatments allow AIDS patients to live longer lives of quality and dignity. Unfortunately, our treatments only slow the progression of AIDS. Eventually the HIV virus will win and AIDS patients will die, often in the prime of their lives.

We have learned an important lesson about our bodies from those who have suffered with this disease. The immune system is essential for our survival. It protects us from infection, it controls certain types of cancer, and as a result, we live longer, healthier, happier lives.

CONDITION TWO—WHEN THE IMMUNE SYSTEM OVER FUNCTIONS: ALLERGIC REACTIONS AND AUTOIMMUNITY

Allergic Reactions

Clearly, we need our immune system. Without it we could not survive for long, but there are times when the immune system harms us rather than helps us. If you suffer from watery eyes, sneezing, and a stuffy nose every spring or fall, your doctor may have told you that you have hay fever. This is an allergic reaction to pollen, dust, or spores that are present in the air. Your immune system attacks these foreign materials, and the result is swollen and itchy tissue in the nose and eyes. Another example of the immune system working against you is a reaction to poison ivy (Figure 1.3). This plant secretes an oil that is very reactive to our immune systems. When the oil gets on your skin, you get a localized reaction that results in a red rash and itching. This too is due to your immune system.

Autoimmunity

The cases in the preceding paragraph are bothersome but seldom life-threatening. There are other conditions where the immune system causes problems that are much more serious. One of the wonderful and amazing things about the immune system is that it can tell the difference between our own cells and tissues and those that are "foreign." The

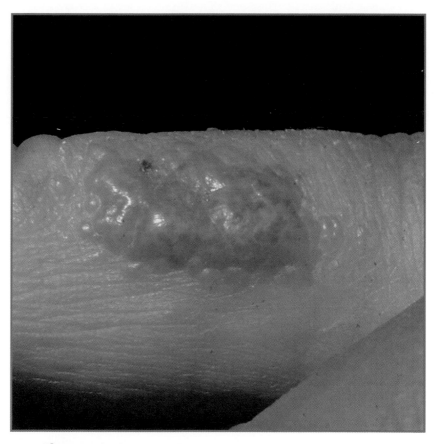

Figure 1.3 Plants such as poison ivy, poison oak, and poison sumac contain a large molecule called urishiol. This large molecule is secreted from the plant as an oil. Urishiol contains many different epitopes, or antigenic sites. As a result, almost everyone is allergic to these plants. As with most allergic reactions on the skin, the poison ivy group oils cause a localized reaction, resulting in reddening of the skin, the presence of a raised rash, and itching (pictured here). Poison ivy cannot be transferred from person to person, but it can be picked up from clothing that is contaminated with the oil.

ability of our body to attack foreign materials, but not our own, is due to a function known as suppression. The body suppresses immune reactions against our own cells but attacks other things, such as bacteria, viruses, and even cancer cells. Sometimes, however, our immune system does not recognize our own tissues and will begin attacking those tissues. Children with juvenile diabetes have a genetic defect that allows the immune system to attack the cells in the pancreas that produce insulin. Insulin is a hormone that is essential for maintaining the proper level of sugar in our blood. Without insulin, diabetics cannot use sugar properly and as a result, they can become very ill or even die when the sugar levels are too high.

Once these insulin-producing cells are destroyed by the immune system, usually around age five or six, the diabetic person must take regular injections of insulin to maintain normal levels of sugar in the blood. Sometimes a diabetic patient will have to take several insulin injections a day, and he must be careful not to give himself too much insulin as this can also lead to death. Juvenile diabetes, also called Type I, or insulin-dependent diabetes, is called an "autoimmune" disease because the immune system attacks its own body. Other examples of autoimmune diseases are rheumatoid arthritis, a disease where the immune system attacks the soft tissues that line and cushion the joints, and lupus, a disease where the immune system attacks the connective tissue of our skin. Later in this book we will explore autoimmune diseases and other health problems caused by the immune system in more detail.

CONNECTIONS

What can we learn from these two very different problems with the immune system? On the one hand, the immune system under functions due to damage of critical cells by a virus. On the other hand we have conditions where our immune system attacks our own bodies, making us sick and potentially resulting in death. The fact that the immune system functions normally for the vast majority of people indicates that it has evolved to be very finely tuned and to function optimally. The remaining chapters in this book will help you to understand just how the immune system works. It is an intricate and elegant system that is essential for our survival. Your journey to understanding the immune system has just begun. As we explore it in greater detail you will see why many scientists consider it to be the most complex and surprising system in the human body. Welcome to the world of multiple tissues, cells, and proteins, choreographed into the complex dance that is the immune system.

2

Innate Immunity and Defenses

GENERAL TYPES OF INNATE IMMUNITY

In some of the subsequent chapters of this book we will learn about the amazingly complex immune system of the human body. Some of the immune responses are so specific they can easily distinguish one bacterium from another or one cell type from another. This specific form of immunity is often referred to as the **acquired immune system** because we only activate it when we are first exposed to a foreign germ or to a vaccine. This ability to mount an attack against a specific foreign invader is one of the most fascinating and complex processes of our bodies. As important as these acquired reactions are, there is another aspect of our defense against germs that is just as important. This collection of protective defenses is referred to as the innate or natural defense mechanisms. The **innate immune system** is always turned on and defends us against harmful things our bodies have never seen before. These innate or natural defenses are so important we could not live without them.

We will discuss these innate defense mechanisms in two categories. The first, the **passive, barrier defenses**, protect us by preventing the entry of harmful things such as bacteria, fungi, viruses, and toxins, into the deeper tissues of our bodies where they could do a great deal of damage. These barrier defenses perform the same function as a moat and the reinforced walls that surround a castle (see box on p. 25). Their purpose is to keep the enemy out. The second category of innate mechanism is the **non-specific, reactive responses**.

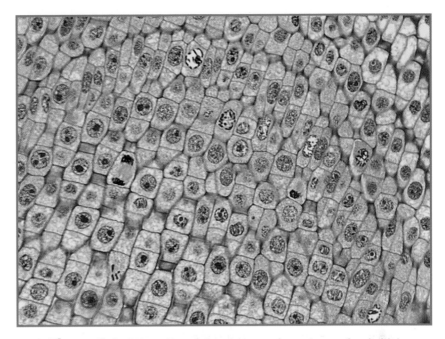

Figure 2.1 Skin cells, pictured here, are made up of cuboidal (cube-shaped) epithelial cells. These cells pack together tightly, keeping moisture in the body and preventing microorganisms from entering into deeper tissues. Your intact skin layer is your first and one of your best defenses against infection. Infections most often occur when the skin is damaged by abrasions or cuts.

These defenses aggressively attack foreign material that invades the body. Using our castle analogy, these defenses would be the equivalent of the soldiers that fight back the invaders that manage to get past the barrier defenses. As you will see, these fighting soldiers have an extensive arsenal of weapons they can use to keep the invaders out.

Barrier Defenses

The barrier defenses are those layers on the outer surface of the body that protect the deeper tissues. The skin is one of the most important barrier defenses, and the largest organ of the body. It is made up of cells called **epithelial cells** (Figure 2.1). The design of the skin is critical to its role as a barrier. First of all, the epithelial cells are very geometric in shape. They fit together with virtually no spaces between the cells, making the layers of the skin very impermeable or hard to penetrate. Since the gaps between the cells are so small, even microorganisms cannot pass between skin cells. A second aspect of skin structure that is important is its multi-layered nature. The layers cover each other, and the newest layers are toward the inside of the body. As a skin layer moves toward the outside, it ages and eventually the cells in that layer die. In fact, the outermost layer of your skin is covered with dried, dead cells that you continuously shed. If a microorganism found a way to attach itself to the outer surface of your skin, it would attach to dead skin cells that would fall away, consequently, the microorganism would probably be shed before it could enter the body.

The second barrier defense that is important is the **mucous membranes**. These membranes are found lining the tracts of the body (the respiratory tract, the digestive tract, etc.). Mucous membranes are also made of epithelial cells, but of a different sort than skin. Skin is designed to be impermeable, that is, so nothing can get through it. In order for the body to get nutrients, fluids, and oxygen, and to dispose of urine and fecal material, membranes must be selectively permeable. Consequently, the membranes are made of epithelial cells that are more loosely packed than are skin epithelial cells. By design it would be much easier for foreign objects to cross the membranes, especially small objects like **microorganisms**, but the membranes have another feature that acts as a barrier to foreign objects. Throughout the mucous membranes are specialized cells called goblet cells. These cells produce and secrete a sticky, thick liquid (**mucus**) onto the surface of the membranes. The mucus keeps the membranes moist, but it also acts to trap foreign objects (dust, soot, and microorganisms.) The mucus is similar to fly paper. These objects become trapped in the gooey, sticky mucus and cannot get down to the surface of the membrane itself. Other cells that line the mucous membranes act like little brooms to sweep the mucus and its trapped material toward the exits of the body. Thus, the mucous membranes also serve as a strong barrier to keep foreign objects out of the deeper tissues.

PROTECTING THE KINGDOM

The immune system can be thought as of as an army defending a kingdom (the body). Using this analogy, suppose that you are the leader of the army and that the king has just been killed in a fierce battle which was the result of an attack by an invading army. The invading army destroyed the castle, the surrounding village, and the homes of your people. While the king and his soldiers valiantly held back the invading army, you managed to lead the people out of the kingdom and into the mountains nearby. You know it is your responsibility to rebuild the kingdom. To do this, you must select a new site for the village and must begin building the fortress to defend the castle and its people from future invaders.

At the base of the mountains is a big canyon. The walls of the canyon are steep on three sides and impossible to scale. In the canyon is a fast-moving spring that provides a source of water that can be diverted in front of the canyon to make a moat. The mouth of the canyon opens onto a fertile plain that will provide productive farmland. In short, you have an ideal spot. You set your masons to work cutting blocks from the granite of the mountain, and you have them construct two high walls across the mouth of the canyon. The moat and the walls create a barrier that will resist attacks from the outside. Next you must set to work training soldiers. You will need archers and swordsmen to defend the fortress. Soon you have established a new home for your people: one large enough that all can retreat into it if there are signs of danger and one strong enough to repel any attack. You have served your people well. The human immune system protects the body like a kingdom to keep it safe and keep out invaders.

Because of the continuous barrier created by the skin and mucous membranes, most harmful microorganisms (bacteria, fungi, protozoa, and viruses) are kept on the surface of the body or lining the cavities of the body within the mucous membranes. These areas are often teeming with micro-organisms, while the tissue below these barriers, the internal organs, muscles, blood, etc., are generally sterile (free of microorganisms) in healthy individuals.

There are areas of the body that are not protected by the skin/mucous membrane barrier. The eyes are soft tissues of the body that are exposed to the outside without protection from skin or mucous membranes. The eyes cannot be covered by these layers because if they were, you would not be able to see. Your eyes have developed their own unique forms of defense. In the inside corners of your eyes, near the nose, there are small openings called **tear ducts**. The tear ducts continually secrete tears. The tears are constantly washing the eyes, removing microorganisms before they can penetrate into the soft tissue of the eyeball. A second important defense for the eyes is an enzyme, **lysozyme**, which is secreted with tears. Lysozyme is an enzyme that attacks bacterial cell walls, making those walls weak and causing the bacterial cells to lyse, or rupture. Between the flushing action of tears and the high concentrations of lysozyme, the eyes are well protected and seldom become infected unless a large load of foreign material is introduced into them at one time.

Non-Specific, Reactive Responses

Although the barrier defenses are very effective, sometimes foreign materials will manage to get around the protective barrier and will enter the deeper tissues. These tissues are usually warm, nutrient-rich environments that allow microorganisms to rapidly multiply. Our bodies have developed additional general defense mechanisms to deal with microbes that manage to make it to the deeper tissues. Generally, these defenses are active, aggressive ones. They seek out the invading foreigner and eliminate it. In the remainder of this chapter we will explore several of these defenses. We refer to them as non-specific, reactive responses. They are non-specific because they typically attack anything that is recognized as foreign. They are reactive because they actively attempt to remove foreign material.

Inflammatory Response

The inflammatory response is a complex series of reactions that almost always occurs when foreign material enters the deeper tissues of the body. We can illustrate the important parts of the inflammatory response through a specific example that you have probably experienced. Imagine you are on a farm and you decide to climb from the first floor of the barn into the hayloft. You reach for the wooden ladder that is made of unfinished wood and as your hand slides along the rung you feel a sharp stick. When you look at your palm you see that a small splinter of wood has come off the rung of the ladder and is now below the surface of your skin. You cannot get the splinter out, but since it does not hurt too much you decide to continue to explore the barn. Soon you forget that the splinter is in your palm.

The next morning you get out of bed and head downstairs, but as you grasp the handrail of the stairs, you feel a throbbing pain in your hand. When you look at your palm you see that the area around the splinter is swollen and red. As you touch it gently with your finger, you find that it is warmer than the rest of your hand and that it is sore. Your palm is displaying the classic symptoms of an inflammatory response (Figure 2.2).

Inflammation results in swelling, redness, heat, and soreness. All of these symptoms are the result of increased blood flow to the wounded area and to the leakage of fluid from the blood into the tissues around the wound. What causes these symptoms to occur? When cells are damaged, as are the cells that were penetrated by the splinter, they release chemicals

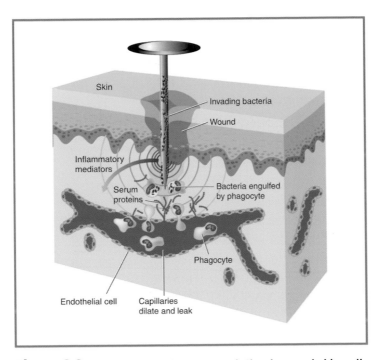

Figure 2.2 When the skin is penetrated, the damaged skin cells release inflammatory mediators that begin the acute inflammatory response. Chemicals on the surface of bacteria and other infectious organisms that have been introduced into the wound also serve as inflammatory mediators. These inflammatory mediators increase dilation of blood vessels in the area, causing fluids and cells from the circulatory system to infuse the tissues around the wound. This causes the injured site to become warm, red, and swollen. The swelling stimulates nerve endings in the area, resulting in pain. The inflammatory mediators also serve to attract immune-active cells to the site so these cells can begin to fight any potential infection.

known as **inflammatory mediators**. The outer surfaces of many bacteria also contain chemicals that serve as inflammatory mediators, and the splinter that penetrated through the protective barrier of your skin probably contained millions of bacteria. These inflammatory mediators have two important functions. First, they cause the capillaries in the area of the wound to dilate or become leaky. Fluid seeps from the circulatory system into the tissues around the wounded site. This results in the swelling that occurs. Since the fluid is mostly water, and since water holds heat well, the increase in fluid also accounts for the heat you feel at the site. The redness results from movement of blood cells into the affected area. The pain is the result of the extra fluid increasing pressure at the site, which stimulates pressure-sensitive nerves. The second function of inflammatory mediators is to recruit other cells that are important in the immune response.

Inflammation has several benefits. First, the buildup of fluid may actually push the splinter out of the wound. This eliminates many of the bacteria and reduces the chance for infection. Second, as the fluid leaks into the site, it brings with it proteins called **antibodies**. These antibodies attach to foreign materials and act as tags for both white blood cells and a class of proteins called complement proteins. Antibodies will be discussed more in depth in later chapters. Both will ultimately eliminate bacteria from the site. Third, as the capillaries become leaky, phagocytic white blood cells leave the circulatory system and enter the tissues. These cells then engulf foreign materials and chemically destroy them.

Inflammation almost always occurs when there is injury or infection to the human body. For example, when you get a sore throat, it becomes hot and red because the tissues become inflamed. As the tissues swell, the opening of the throat gets smaller. This is why it is often hard to swallow when you have a sore throat. In almost all cases when you are sick or injured and when the area that is affected becomes sore, it is the result of inflammation.

PHAGOCYTIC CELLS

Phagocytic cells are a subgroup of the white blood cells, or leukocytes. Phagocytic means "cell eating." These cells travel through the tissues of the body and search for foreign materials, including microorganisms. When they find something that should not be there, the phagocytic cell will attach to the foreign material and will push its cell membrane out like two small hands on either side of the foreign material, grasping it as you might a butterfly with your cupped hands. This process is called **phagocytosis** (Figure 2.3). The membrane of the phagocytic cell then fuses to trap the foreign material inside a sphere of membrane called a phagosome. This is like a bubble inside the cell. There are other bubble-like structures inside the phagocytic cell that contain very powerful enzymes and chemicals. The cell will fuse these chemical- or enzyme-containing bubbles to the phagosome so that the contents of the two mix. The result is that the enzymes and chemicals destroy the foreign material. If that foreign material is a microorganism, the chemical or enzyme treatment kills it and makes it fall apart. This prevents it from reproducing in the body and therefore avoids infection.

You have phagocytic white blood cells in virtually all tissues of your body, but some tissues have more than others. For instance, your lungs are one site in the body where the mucous membranes have to be relatively thin and free of mucus. This is essential because the tiny pockets in your lungs, the alveoli, are the site where oxygen and carbon dioxide are exchanged in the blood. If the membranes were too thick, or if the layer of mucus were too heavy, you would not get good gas exchange in the lungs. The lungs have large numbers of specialized phagocytes called alveolar macrophages in the alveoli, the small sacks in the lungs where oxygen and carbon dioxide gases exchange between the air and the blood. **Macrophage** means a big, eating cell. These alveolar macrophages move throughout the alveoli engulfing and destroying any foreign material, including microorganisms that may make it into the deepest parts of the lungs. You will also find large numbers of phagocytic cells in the **lymphatic tissues**, including the tonsils and the lymph nodes. We will discuss these lymphatic tissues and organs in the next chapter.

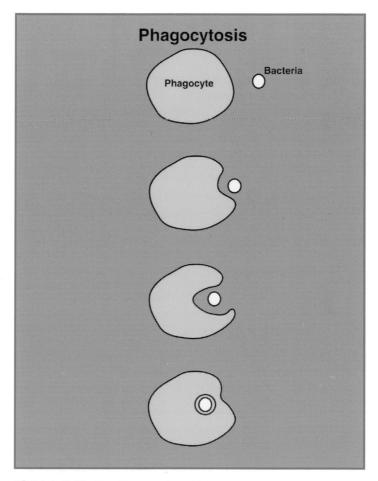

Figure 2.3 Certain cells, including macrophages and a number of other white blood cells, respond to the presence of antibodies on the surface of a foreign material or react with binding sites on the foreign materials themselves. These cells are called phagocytic cells. This recognition of the attached antibodies or binding sites causes the cells to bind the foreign material. The phagocytic cell then extends its cell membrane around both sides of the foreign material until the two "arms" of the cell meet. These arms fuse together, trapping the foreign material in a special vesicle called a "phagosome." The phagosome then fuses with other vesicles in the phagocytic cell that contain powerful enzymes and chemicals. These enzymes and chemicals break down the foreign materials into small pieces.

In addition to phagocytic cells, the body contains other immune-active cells that are attracted to infected tissues, but we will discuss these in more detail later.

COMPLEMENT PROTEINS

One of the most interesting and complicated of the non-specific, reactive defenses is the **complement system. Complement proteins** are found in the blood. While we do not know the exact number, there may be as many as 60 different proteins that make up the complement system. These proteins work through a sequential, or cascade, reaction. One or a few of the complement proteins acts first; then another group will be activated, then another, and another, until finally the foreign material is destroyed. Complement proteins seem to be most important in fighting bacterial infections, but unlike antibodies, which are also proteins found in the blood, complement proteins do not differentiate between bacteria, whereas antibodies generally only attack a single, specific bacterial species. There are several different complement pathways. The two we will mention here are the **classical complement pathway** and the **alternate complement pathway**.

The classical complement pathway (Figure 2.4) requires the involvement of antibodies. When antibodies bind to a microorganism, such as a bacterium, sections of the antibody protein extend away from the bacterial cell. One of the complement proteins can bind to the free ends of the antibody molecule and once bound to the antibody molecule, the complement protein changes shape and becomes the binding site for different complement proteins. These new complement proteins bind to the first protein, and the new proteins split. One piece remains attached to the bacterial cell while the other floats away and becomes both an **inflammatory mediator** and an attracting agent for immune system cells. The fragments of the second round of complement proteins bind and alter other complement proteins. These proteins embed into the wall of

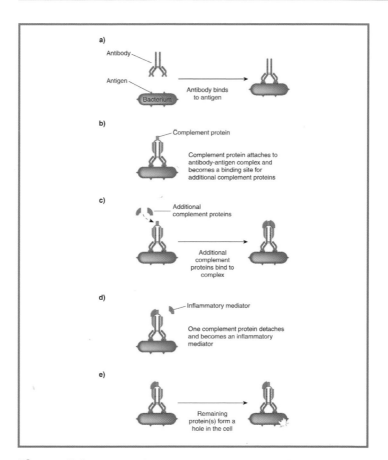

Figure 2.4 The classical complement pathway, illustrated here, works in cooperation with the humoral immune system. IgG antibodies bind to antigens on the surface of foreign cells, such as bacterial cells. Once bound by its variable region, the antibody molecule extends its constant region away from the foreign cell. One of the many complement proteins binds to the constant region of the attached IgG and becomes cleaved, or broken, into pieces. One of these pieces remains attached to the antibody molecule and serves to attract additional complement proteins. The other fragments of the first complement proteins are released and serve to recruit additional complement proteins to the site of the infection. These fragments also serve as inflammatory mediators. Eventually several different complement proteins will bind to the foreign cell and create a hole in the wall or membrane of that cell. This results in lysis of the cell and its destruction.

the bacterial cell and eventually form a hole in the cell. The hole is completely surrounded by a ring of complement proteins. Once this hole is formed, fluids rush into the bacterial cell, causing it to explode.

The alternate complement pathway results in the same fate: the formation of a ring of complement proteins which create a hole in the bacterial cell. That results in lysis (bursting) and killing of the cell, but the alternate pathway does not require antibody molecules. There are specific molecules on the surface of certain bacterial cells that will bind complement proteins on their own. Once these proteins bind, they start the complement cascade of binding and splitting complement proteins until the complement ring punches a hole in the bacterial cells, resulting in their deaths.

In addition to punching holes in bacterial cells, fragments of some complement proteins act as inflammatory mediators, causing capillaries to dilate and allowing fluid and cells from the circulatory system to enter the site where the bacteria are found. Some of the fragments that stick to the bacterial cells serve to attract and activate phagocytosis by macrophages.

The role of complement in protecting us from infection is best understood by observing people with defective complement systems. Some individuals are born with genetic defects that prevent them from making one or more of the complement proteins. These individuals are much more susceptible to certain bacterial infections and, as a result, are sick more often than people with normal complement systems. As a group, people born with defective complement systems are more likely to die from certain bacterial infections than those who have function- ing complement systems.

THE CONSEQUENCE OF INNATE IMMUNITY

As you can see, our innate or non-specific defenses are very important in helping us to avoid infections or to fight foreign microorganisms before they have a chance to establish an infection. The combination of the barrier defenses, along with the non-specific, reactive defenses is usually effective in helping us avoid infectious diseases. Unfortunately, sometimes these innate defenses are not quite enough, and infectious microorganisms make it into our bodies and begin to grow. The next chapter will identify some of the important cells, tissues, and organs of our bodies that fight back when these infectious microorganisms make it past our innate defenses.

CONNECTIONS

In this chapter we have seen that the body has a number of "general" or innate immune defenses. The skin and mucous membranes serve as a protective barrier to keep foreign organisms out of the more sensitive body areas. This defense works much as do the moat and defensive walls of a castle. When foreign organisms breach these defenses, the body has other general defenses. The inflammatory response is a generalized reaction to anything foreign or to damage to cells. Either the foreign organism or the damaged tissues themselves send out inflammatory mediators that cause the compromised area to flood with fluids, bringing in a huge number of proteins and defensive cells to ward off the invaders.

Among those cells brought to the site are macrophages and other phagocytic cells. These cells engulf foreign microorganisms, subjecting the microbes to a series of powerful chemicals and enzymes that lead to their destruction. Finally, we learned about the complement system, a series of proteins found in blood serum that sets off a chain reaction that ultimately leads to proteins creating holes in the invading cells, allowing the influx of water which causes the cell to lyse. Like any good defense plan, the innate immune system has backup after backup, ensuring that most invaders are dealt with before they can cause harm.

3

The Cells, Tissues, and Organs of the Immune System

THE DIVERSITY OF THE IMMUNE SYSTEM

Unlike some of the other systems of the body, it is not easy to recognize all of the players of the immune system (Figure 3.1). While there are three basic types of muscles, they all share certain characteristics and it is easy to see that they make up a cohesive muscular system. Likewise, while bones come in all shapes and sizes, they are more alike than they are different and as a result, the skeletal system is fairly easy to identify. The immune system, on the other hand, is made of a wide and assorted array of components. Some of these components exist as single cells. Others are specific sets of tissues, similar cells that form a mass with a like appearance and function. Still others are complex organs. As we will learn in this chapter, we find parts of the immune system throughout the body, and we often mistake these as parts of other body systems.

In fact, in some cases the components of the immune system are integral parts of other systems of the body. In this chapter we will begin to identify the players in the immune system. We will not delve into their specific functions in detail here. We will see how these components function, either alone or together, in later chapters in the book. For the sake of convenience, we will cluster these various immune system components into four categories. These categories

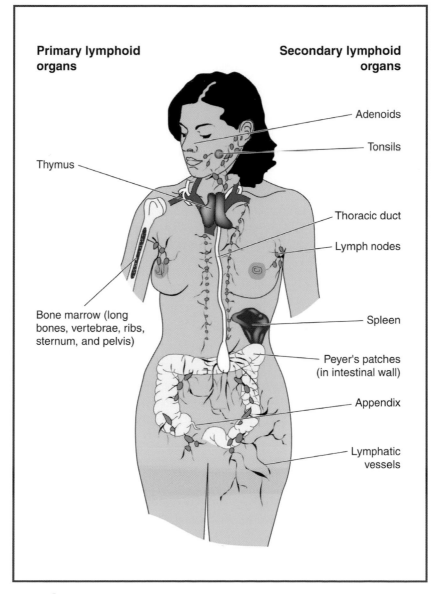

Primary lymphoid organs

Thymus

Bone marrow (long bones, vertebrae, ribs, sternum, and pelvis)

Secondary lymphoid organs

Adenoids

Tonsils

Thoracic duct

Lymph nodes

Spleen

Peyer's patches (in intestinal wall)

Appendix

Lymphatic vessels

Figure 3.1 The immune system consists of a number of organs, tissues, and vessels. The organs of the immune system include the primary organs, the thymus and the bone marrow, where immune-active cells are made or mature. The secondary organs, including the tonsils, adenoids, spleen, lymph nodes, and others, are sites where immune active cells focus their activity, that is, they are the sites where the various cells of the immune system attack and destroy foreign materials.

are individual cells, tissues, organs, and multi-organ systems. We will begin our exploration with the most basic of these classes, the individual cells.

INDIVIDUAL CELL TYPES IMPORTANT TO THE IMMUNE SYSTEM

The most important individual cells of the immune system are all **white blood cells** (Figure 3.2). Although these cells are very different in appearance and function, they are all derived from the same source; in fact, all blood cells are generated from this source. The tissue of the body where blood cells are made is red bone marrow, the soft central core found in many of the long bones of the human body. Within the bone marrow are a group of special cells, called stem cells. These cells are called undifferentiated cells because they can give rise to different types of final cells. Once a cell differentiates, it can only make additional copies of itself when it undergoes mitosis, but an undifferentiated cell can divide and generate multiple types of cells. The process of making blood cells is called **hemopoiesis**. Hemopoiesis gives rise to the **erythrocytes**, or red blood cells, which are vital in transporting oxygen and carbon dioxide through the body, and the **leukocytes**, or white blood cells, which are critical for the immune response. You may have also learned that platelets are a type of blood cell. Actually, platelets are fragments of blood cells, not intact cells themselves, but they too are derived from the stem cells of red bone marrow. Since our focus is on the immune system, we will dispense with further discussion of erythrocytes and platelets here and will focus on the leukocytes.

As bone marrow stem cells begin to divide, they can differentiate into a major precursor cell class called the leukocytes. Leukocytes further differentiate into two major classes: the phagocytic family and the lymphoid family. The phagocyte precursor cell can then differentiate further. Two derivatives of this cell are the **mononuclear leukocytes** and the **polymorphonuclear leukocytes** (granulated leukocytes). These long,

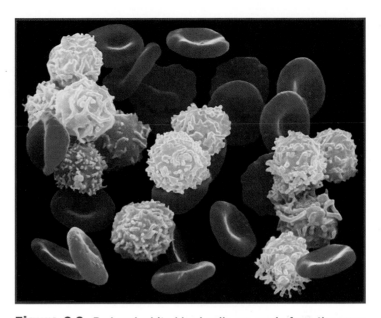

Figure 3.2 Red and white blood cells are made from the same stem cells found in the marrow of long bones. Red blood cells are primarily involved in gas transport, taking oxygen from the lungs to the tissues, and carbon dioxide from the tissues to the lungs. White blood cells are much more diverse and are usually involved in the various processes of the immune system. As you can see in the figure, red blood cells are shaped like disks with a depressed center. These cells do not contain a nucleus and therefore do not have substantial amounts of DNA in them. White blood cells have a number of appearances and all contain nuclei.

technical names may seem a little intimidating, but if you break them down into the meanings of their root components, you can actually learn a great deal about the nature of the cells. For the mononuclear leukocytes, "mono" means "one" and "nuclear" means "nucleus." All of these cells have a single nucleus in them. We also refer to these cells as agranulocytes because they do not contain granules of special proteins or chemicals in special organelles of the cytoplasm. All mononuclear leukocytes develop into a special type of cell called a **monocyte**. Monocytes make up about 8% of all leukocytes in the blood. Later, some of these monocytes can further differentiate into another cell type important in fighting infection, the macrophages. Macrophages are not found in the bloodstream itself, but seem to develop from monocytes as the monocytes squeeze through the walls of capillaries and move into the fluids that bathe the tissues of the body.

The polymorphonuclear leukocytes are more complex. The name tells us something about their function. "Poly" means "many," "morpho" means "shape," and "nuclear" means "nucleus." Thus these cells have different shapes for their nuclei. These precursors develop into one of three types of cells. **Neutrophils** are polymorphonuclear leukocytes that have neutral granules, "neutral" meaning no net charge. These cells stain poorly because most of the dyes used to stain human cells do so through charged groups on the stain surface. Since the neutrophils are neutral in charge they do not bind stains well. The neutrophils are the largest class of polymorphonuclear leukocytes, constituting more than 50% of all leukocytes.

A second class of this family is the **eosinophil**. Eosin is a red dye that has a net, negative charge; thus, the granules of eosinophils which have a net positive charge will bind this dye. Eosinophil means "eosin loving." While the eosinophils make up only a small part of the total leukocyte population in the blood, about 6%, they are very important in fighting infections by fungi, protozoa, and worms.

The final group of polymorphonuclear leukocytes is the **basophils**. Basophils contain granules made of compounds with a net negative charge; consequently they bind positively charged dyes, which are also called basic dyes. Methylene blue is one such dye and when added to a blood smear, basophils will bind the methylene blue, taking on a blue color for their granules. The basophils are the least numerous of the leukocytes, making up less than 1% of total leukocytes in the blood. Basophils seem to be closely related to another group of cells, called mast cells. Both basophils and mast cells contain a compound called histamine.

When activated, these cells release their histamine, resulting in an inflammatory reaction. Basophils and mast cells are directly involved in allergic reactions, which is why we will often take antihistamines to fight the symptoms of allergies (stuffiness, runny nose, etc.). Antihistamines block the action of histamine.

The second major family of leukocytes derived from bone marrow stem cells is the **lymphoid** family. Depending on where in the body these cells mature, they will develop into one of two cell types. When the lymphoid precursor cell remains in the bone marrow to mature, it becomes a B lymphocyte, or **B cell**. B cells are the principal cells for making antibodies. We will discuss this process in a later chapter. When the lymphoid precursor migrates to the thymus, a gland that lies in front of the heart, the precursor becomes one of a number of types of T lymphocytes, or **T cells**. T cells mediate a process known as **cell-mediated immunity**. They are also critical in regulating the intensity of the immune reaction. There are three major divisions of T cells. **Cytotoxic T cells** (T_C cells) carry out cell-mediated immunity. T helper cells (T_H cells) are central in activating immune responses, and **T suppressor cells** (T_S cells) reduce the intensity of the immune system and also probably play an important role in helping our bodies distinguish our own tissues and cells from those of invading materials.

A third class of lymphoid cells that is less well understood is the Non-B, Non-T, or **Null lymphocytes**. These cells can be distinguished from B and T cells by the absence of certain surface structures. They tend to fight infections, but do so non-specifically. B cells and cytotoxic T cells are programmed to only attack very specific foreign antigens.

THE TISSUES OF THE IMMUNE SYSTEM

In addition to the cells that directly fight infection or regulate the immune process, there are also clusters of similar cells that form tissues critical for immunity. The tonsils are a ring of lymphoid tissue located at the back of the mouth, just at the top of the throat. It is your tonsils that your doctor or nurse will "swab" with a sterile applicator when they are checking for strep throat. A closely related tissue found in the nose is the adenoids. These patches of tissue are positioned where the nasal area opens into the throat. The tonsils and the adenoids are rich with all types of leukocytes. When a foreign organism

WORDS FOR THOUGHT— A GENERATION GAP

Our understanding of the human body is constantly changing. We have learned more about how our bodies function in the past 25 years than we did in all of recorded history prior to that time. As we learn new things, our practice of medicine changes. An important change in medicine occurred between the time your parents or grandparents were children and the time when you and your friends were young. For example, it is very likely that you still have your tonsils. While your parents may have them, their parents probably do not.

Until we began to understand the role of all of the cells, tissues, and organs of the immune system, we did not know how important our tonsils were in fighting infection. The doctors who treated your parents or grandparents considered the tonsils basically useless, and when children of those generations had recurring sore throats, it was common practice to remove the tonsils. We now know that the tonsils are one of several tissues that are a part of the immune system and that they help to fight infection. In fact, the recurring sore throats associated with the tonsils are due to the fact that the body will isolate harmful microorganisms in the tonsilar tissues where the power of the immune system can be directed at the elimination of the invading organisms. Since this results in triggering normal immune responses in the tonsils, they become inflamed—and appear to be infected.

The tonsils help our bodies fight infection, and thus doctors are reluctant to remove them from patients unless the chronic (recurring) sore throats are threatening the health of the person. As we now know that the tonsils are important to our health, you are more likely to keep yours.

enters the body through the mouth or nose, it is usually transported to either the tonsils or adenoids where the cells of the immune system launch an attack. We have only learned the important role these tissues play in preventing infections that enter through the respiratory system in recent years. Now that we know the critical role the tonsils and adenoids play in fighting infection, doctors are much more hesitant to remove them.

Another important mass of lymphoid tissue is the appendix (Figure 3.3). As with the tonsils, it was much more common to remove a person's appendix a generation or two ago because we did not know its function. We assumed that it was unessential and therefore, if it became inflamed (which would not be unusual for a lymphoid tissue) we thought it could be removed with no ill effects. While we still do not completely understand the role of the appendix, it is probably important in protecting the lower digestive tract and the body cavity from infectious agents that enter the body through food or water.

The final general group of lymphoid tissues is the **Peyer's patches**. Peyer's patches are small pockets of lymphoid tissue found in the intestines. They may play a similar protective role to the appendix. Closely related to Peyer's patches are **skin-associated lymphoid tissue (SALT)** and **mucosal-associated lymphoid tissue (MALT).** These patches of tissue are located below the surface of the skin and mucous membranes, respectively. They are critical in preventing infections that might result if infectious organisms cross these natural barriers. The importance of SALT has been demonstrated in burn patients. Severe burn patients whose SALT patches are intact and functional are much less likely to have their burns become infected than are those whose SALT patches are damaged by the burn.

ORGANS OF THE IMMUNE SYSTEM

An organ is a collection of different tissues that work together to perform one or more important functions. The organs of the immune system can be divided into two major classes. Primary

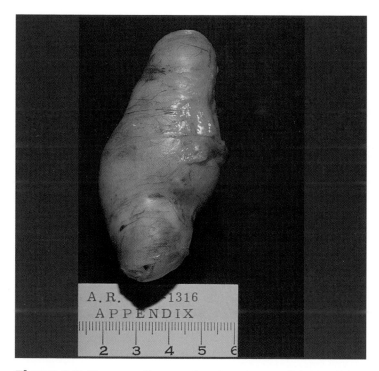

Figure 3.3 The appendix, once thought to be a vestigial (no longer useful) organ, is now known to be an important secondary immune system organ. The appendix is a site where the body delivers foreign invaders, such as infectious bacterial cells, for attack by the immune system. The appendix in the figure is swollen due to the inflammatory response at the site. When the appendix becomes infected, the condition is called appendicitis. It may be necessary to remove the appendix surgically because the inflammation becomes so severe it may rupture and spread infectious bacteria throughout the abdomen, a condition that can be deadly.

lymphoid organs include the bone marrow and the thymus. They are essential for the production and development of the various classes of lymphocytes. Bone marrow is an important primary lymphoid organ. It is the site of blood cell production, including lymphocytes. The bones most important in this process are the vertebrae, the ribs, the sternum, the long bones of the arms and legs, and the pelvis. Bone marrow not only gives rise to all types of blood cells, but it is also the location for the specialization of B cells. The second primary lymphoid organ is the thymus. As mentioned previously, the thymus is a small organ located just in front of the heart. The thymus is critical in the development and maturation of T cells.

The secondary lymphoid organs are the lymph nodes (Figure 3.4) and the spleen. Have you ever noticed that sometimes when you have a sore throat, the "glands" in your neck will swell? Those glands are actually lymph nodes which are fighting infections. Because they activate the immune system within their structure, the tissues of the lymph nodes become inflamed and sore. Lymph nodes are scattered throughout the body, but especially along the neck and trunk. There are significant concentrations of lymph nodes in the area of the hip joint, along the abdomen, under the sternum and around the breasts, and under the arms and into the neck. The word "node" means a point of connection. The lymph nodes are the locations where various branches of the lymphatic system come together. We will discuss the lymphatic system in the final section of this chapter.

In addition to the lymph nodes, the spleen is another very important secondary lymphatic organ. The spleen is located in the upper part of the abdomen, just below the diaphragm. The spleen is fed by a large number of blood vessels, and, as a result, the blood spends a significant amount of time in the spleen. Unfortunately, the spleen is not very well protected by the body. It is not unusual when a person has a serious blow to the abdomen, as one might experience in a serious automobile accident, a fall, or a crushing blow, for the spleen to rupture. Since so much blood flows through the spleen, a rupture of the spleen can cause massive internal bleeding, and, as a result, it may have to be removed to prevent the victim from bleeding to death. Fortunately, this is fairly routine surgery, and most patients recover from a spleenectomy. Unfortunately, without a spleen, these individuals typically suffer from many more infections than persons with a functional spleen, indicating the importance of this organ in immune defense.

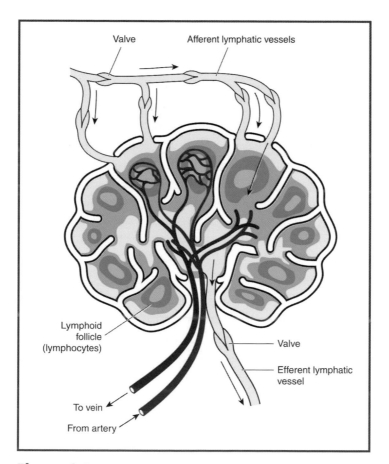

Figure 3.4 Lymph nodes, shown here, are small secondary immune organs that are found at the intersections of lymphatic vessels. These nodes attract and retain phagocytic cells and other immune-active cells. They are often sites where infecting bacteria are attacked. In certain infections, the lymph nodes become so inflamed they swell and become extremely painful. Lymph nodes also capture cancer cells that are released from tumors.

LYMPHATIC CIRCULATION

We tend to think of the circulatory system as a closed loop of tubes, arteries, capillaries, and veins, which transport blood from the heart to the lungs and to the body. However, the circulatory system is not absolutely closed. The fluid of the blood, the plasma, can and does seep through the walls of blood vessels, mainly the capillary walls, and bathes the tissues in fluid. Once the fluid leaves the circulatory system and enters the tissues it is referred to as lymph. Additionally, monocytes, one of the classes of white blood cells, can also squeeze through the walls of the capillaries when signaled to do so. When they do, these cells undergo another transformation and become **macrophages**. "Macro" means "large" and "phage" means "to eat," thus, macrophages are large polymorphonuclear leukocytes that wander around the tissues looking for foreign invaders. When they find them, they will engulf the proteins, bacteria, viruses, or whatever these foreign invaders happen to be and destroy them. Moreover, they will actually use pieces of these destroyed materials to activate the immune system to fight even harder. Obviously, if the fluid from the circulatory system gets out into the tissues, there has to be a way to close the loop and return it to the bloodstream. The fluids around the tissue drain into collection tubes called lymphatic vessels. These lymphatic vessels merge at intersections marked by lymph nodes. Ultimately all of the lymphatic vessels and lymph nodes merge into the final component of lymphatic circulation, the thoracic duct. This duct empties the lymph from the lymphatic system into the heart, thus returning the fluid back into the circulatory system.

CONNECTIONS

You can see from this chapter that the immune system is a very complicated and essential system of the human body. It involves the action of individual cells, specific tissues, immune system essential organs, and a fluid management system that is separate from, but permanently linked to, the circulatory system. Unless these players work together, the body's ability to fight infection is compromised. In later chapters, we will explore some of the specific ways these players work together to protect our bodies from infections and sometimes from its own cells.

4

The Humoral Immune Response

THE BASIC UNIT OF HUMORAL IMMUNITY —
THE ANTIBODY

The **humoral immune system** is a powerful defense against foreign materials (bacteria, viruses, fungi, toxins, etc.) that make it past the barrier defenses and enter into the deeper tissues or the blood stream. The basic functional unit of humoral immunity is a special molecule called the antibody, also called **immunoglobulin**. Antibodies are made of proteins that are joined together and are very specific. The body has five basic types of antibodies. The first antibody type is immunoglobulin G (IgG): the most common antibody type in the blood. The second most common type found in the blood is immunoglobulin M (IgM). IgM is a very large complex that contains five IgG-like molecules joined together in a huge complex. IgM is the form of antibody we make the very first time our immune system is exposed to a new foreign agent. IgA is an antibody type that is made of two IgG-like complexes that are joined together. As long as these two units remained joined together, the IgA molecule can be secreted across the mucous membranes. For this reason, IgA is very important in defending us from infections in areas with lots of membranes. IgA, for instance, is secreted across the mucous membranes of the respiratory system to fight infections of the nose and throat. It also is secreted across the lining of the intestinal tract to defend us from infections of the digestive system.

IgE is a special class of antibody. It is found only in low concentrations and helps to fight parasitic infections (infections by fungi, worms, and protozoa). IgE is shaped like IgG, but has a constant end of the molecule that binds granular white blood cells and mast cells. When these cells bind IgE that has bound an antigen (parts of molecules that bind specifically to antibodies), the granular white blood cells and mast cells degranulate, that is, they release their contents. Among these contents are histamine and other inflammatory mediatators that trigger inflammation.

If you have hay fever, your body makes IgE against certain types of pollen. If you inhale that pollen into the mouth and nose, IgE will bind the pollen antigens, trigger binding of the IgE molecule to the mast cells and granular white blood cells, and will cause histamine release. This causes the tissues in your nose to inflame. The swelling of the tissues makes your nose feel "stuffy" and causes fluid to drain, giving you a runny nose.

The last type of antibody is IgD. IgD is found on the surface of B cells and T cells and serves as the antigen receptor site that triggers cell activation and immune response. For the sake of this chapter, we will limit our discussion of the antibody molecule to IgG, the most common.

The IgG molecule is made up of four proteins. Two are identical large proteins, and the other two are identical smaller proteins. These join together to form a "Y"-shaped molecule (Figure 4.1). The two large proteins form the basic structure of the Y. They are joined together by chemical bonds in the base of the "Y." The ends of the large molecules that make the base are called constant regions. That is, all human IgG molecules have exactly the same amino acids making up this stem, regardless of what antigen binds to that particular antibody. These constant regions continue about halfway up each "arm" of the "Y." The small proteins line the inside of the arms of the "Y." and each is joined with chemical bonds to the upper end of a large protein molecule. As a result, all four proteins are physically bonded to each other and cannot come apart. The half of the small protein

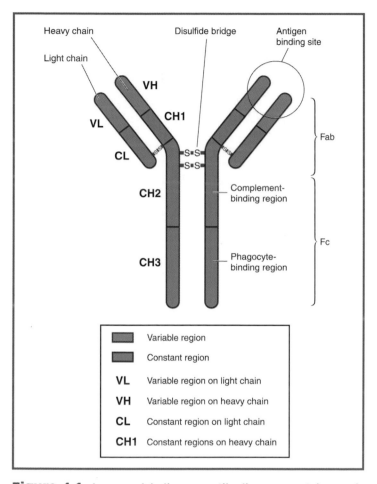

Figure 4.1 Immunoglobulins, or antibodies, are proteins made by B cells. The figure shown here is of immunoglobulin G (IgG), the most common type of immunoglobulin. IgG is made up of two large proteins (heavy chain) and two small proteins (light chain). These proteins join together to form a Y-shaped molecule. The "arms" of the Y are called variable regions. IgG contains two arms, and each of the arms on a given IgG molecule is identical, allowing each IgG to bind two identical antigens. Different B cells produce different IgG molecules. The base of the IgG, the constant region, is always the same, even when antibodies are made by different B cells, but the variable regions are unique for each B cell and each will only bind one specific type of antigen. Other immunoglobulins will have multiple combinations of these "Y" molecules.

molecules toward the base are constant for all IgG molecules. The upper ends of the large and the small proteins that make the tips of the arms are called variable regions. It is these variable regions that make the antibodies specific for binding a given antigen. The shape and charges (positive or negative) of the variable regions determine which antigen the antibody molecule will bind. Since the two upper arms are identical, each IgG molecule has the ability to bind two identical antigens. The same is true for IgE and IgD antibodies; each will bind two identical antigens. Since IgM is made up of five basic subunits and since each binds two antigens, the IgM molecules can bind ten identical antigens at once. IgA is a dimer, made up of two identical antibody units so each IgA molecule can bind four antigens.

The variable regions of the antibodies give them their specificity for their unique antigen. The constant regions are also important because they are recognized by different components of the immune system. Interestingly, while every IgG molecule in a human has the same constant regions, regardless of the antigens it binds, the IgG constant region of a human is different from that of a mouse, or a horse, or a rabbit. Every animal species that makes antibodies has its own unique constant region.

Later we will look at an example of how antibodies are made. The example will discuss the immune response to a bacterial infection. Most foreign cells have many copies of their antigens on their surfaces, perhaps hundreds of copies of those surface antigens. Since each cell has lots of antigens, and each IgG molecules has two antigen binding sites, IgG molecules tend to bind to the surface of bacterial cells by turning the "Y" upside down (Figure 4.2). The arms of the "Y" attach to the cell, each arm to a different copy of the same antigen. When there are multiple bacterial cells present as there almost always are in an infection (there may be thousands or millions of identical bacterial cells), some of the IgG

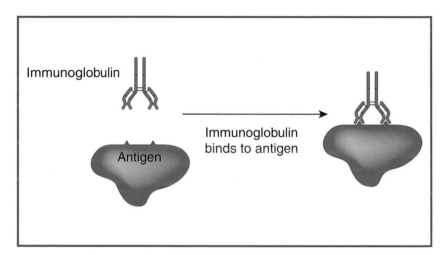

Immunoglobulin

Antigen

Immunoglobulin
binds to antigen

Figure 4.2 Each IgG molecule has two antigen binding sites. Typically, bacteria and other infectious organisms will have multiple copies of key antigens on their surface. An IgG molecule can either bind to two of these identical surface antigens on the same bacterial cell or can bind one surface antigen each on two identical bacterial cells. In the latter case, large complexes of antigens and antibodies will form. Note that the antibody binds to the surface of the bacterial cell by attaching the variable regions to the surface antigens. This, in effect, turns the "Y-shaped" molecule upside down. The constant regions are then available to recruit the complement system or other immune-active cells.

molecules will join two bacterial cells together, that is, one arm of the IgG will bind to an antigen on one cell while the other binds to an identical antigen of another cell. The result is that the antibodies tend to clump the foreign cells together. This clumping concentrates the foreign bacteria into clusters that can be more easily targeted by the immune system.

Recall that IgM has ten antigen binding sites and that we said it is the type of antibody made the first time we are exposed to a foreign antigen. When the body is first exposed to a foreign antigen, the humoral immune system takes about ten days before it is fully up to strength. If the foreign antigen is on a bacterial cell, these cells will be constantly reproducing during those ten days. By the time your immune system can strike back, the numbers of bacteria are very large. Since each IgM can bind ten antigens, these antibody molecules tend to quickly tie up the bacteria into large clumps. This helps our bodies to fight back, but often not before the bacterium (or virus or other agent) has made us sick. When we are exposed to the same microorganism later, our immune system can respond much more quickly, usually in a matter of two to three days. This usually eliminates the microbes before they cause damage and disease. This is why if we have a certain disease, like measles or mumps, we usually only have it one time. Any time we are exposed to the same virus after the first exposure, our immune system responds very quickly and produces lots of IgG antibody. This allows us to fight off the virus before the disease can occur again.

A BIOLOGICAL MYSTERY SOLVED

When we first began to understand how the immune system worked, scientists were faced with a difficult question. We knew from molecular biology that every protein in the body had its own gene. When it became clear that immunoglobulins could be made that can specifically bind to literally thousands of different antigens, molecular biologists wanted to know where all these different genes were stored. There was not enough room on the human chromosomes to accommodate all these different immunoglobulin genes. The idea that the body could make different proteins without having a gene for each protein defied our basic understanding of genetics. How could this be?

When scientists began to isolate and sequence immunoglobulins (determine the specific bases that make the genes) an amazing thing was discovered. In the undifferentiated B cells (those that had just been made from bone marrow stem cells and were not dedicated to make a specific antibody) there were clusters of gene sequences that were interchangeable. The typical immunoglobulin molecule could be divided into three or four distinct sections. Before the B cells differentiated, they had several alternative blocks of DNA for each of these sections of the immunoglobulin gene. These blocks were called "cassettes." To make one complete antibody gene, one cassette

A ONE-TIME EVENT

Measles, mumps, German measles, and chickenpox, once called the common childhood diseases, are diseases rarely seen in the United States these days. In fact, most young Americans will probably never suffer from these diseases. However, things were very different for your parents and grandparents. Most Americans the ages of your parents or grandparents have had at least one, and in many cases, all of these diseases. Interestingly, except for very rare cases, they would have had one or more of the diseases, but only one time each. This is due to a very powerful defense mechanism called the humoral immune system. The humoral immune system produces specialized proteins in the blood called antibodies. Antibodies are incredibly specific. An antibody raised against measles has no effect against mumps, German measles, or chickenpox.

Why did your parents and grandparents have these diseases and you probably did not? Normally our bodies do not produce an antibody against a microorganism unless we are exposed to that microbe. Your parents and grandparents would have been exposed to these diseases and the microbes (all viruses) that caused them. Although these diseases are still very common and are the cause of many deaths and permanent disabilities in other parts of the world, they are very rare in the United States. The United States began an aggressive program to "vaccinate" against childhood diseases about 50 years ago. A **vaccination** is exposure to a form of the virus or a part of the virus that is incapable of causing the full symptoms of the disease, but is was needed for each section of the molecule. By rearranging different cassettes into each of the slots, you could literally get thousands of combinations. This idea may be hard to imagine. Let's think about using a more concrete model.

Suppose you have an entertainment center. You can play cassette tapes, DVDs, CDs, and computer games using the

enough like the viruses to "trick" the body into thinking it has been exposed to these viruses. Most American children receive vaccines for these diseases when they are quite young. The chickenpox vaccine, however, was just recently developed (this may explain why you had chickenpox, but not the other three diseases). These vaccines are required for all children entering school. As a result, virtually no young person in the United States is likely to experience these diseases in the future as long as regular vaccination continues. The vaccines activate the cells that make antibodies against each of the viruses so that the body has a significant number of these antibodies against each virus. When the body is exposed to the viruses, the antibodies direct the immune system to destroy them before the virus can cause disease.

Generally, a person will only have these diseases once. The first time the body is exposed to the disease-causing agent, it cannot respond quickly enough to prevent the virus from causing disease, but it will activate the production of antibodies. If the body is exposed to the viruses in the future, there are enough antibodies and specialized antibody producing cells to overwhelm the viruses when they enter the body. Before vaccines, a first exposure to any of these viruses caused disease, but eventually the immune system kicked in and eliminated or contained the virus. The viruses were not allowed a second chance to cause disease, resulting in a "natural" form of vaccination.

entertainment center. Now let's assume that you have four sets of earphones and you can run the four devices all at the same time so four of your friends can use the entertainment center at once. In your collection of media, you have 30 cassette tapes, 45 CDs, 20 DVDs, and 15 computer games. How many different combinations of things can your friends enjoy at any one time? You can determine the number of combinations by multiplying the numbers of each type of media together. Thirty cassette tapes, multiplied by 45 CDs, multiplied by 20 DVDs, multiplied by fifteen computer games (30 X 45 X 20 X 15) equals 405,000 different combinations!

Now let's take a simple four cassette model for an antibody gene. If we assume that there are about fifteen options for the first cassette position, twenty cassette options for the second, eight cassettes for the third position, and six cassettes for the fourth position (15 X 20 X 8 X 6), mixing and matching these cassettes of DNA can make over 14,000 different antibody genes! Suddenly, instead of needing enough room on the chromosome for 14,000 different proteins (and therefore 14,000 different genes), we can accomplish the same number of antibody combinations with enough DNA to only encode forty-nine (15 + 20 + 8 + 6) cassettes, and since each cassette is only a small part of a gene, this requires very little room on the chromosomes of the human genome.

The only problem with this model is that once a cell is programmed to make a particular antibody, what prevents it from rearranging cassettes? When a B cell matures in the bone marrow, it randomly creates one unique arrangement of four cassettes. Once this is done, it becomes a permanent gene for that B cell, and all the other cassettes are lost. Thus, that B cell, and all the cloned B cells that are made from it will only be able to produce one type of antibody that will recognize only one possible antigen. Since the processes of selecting the cassettes is random in the undifferentiated precursor B cell (the B cell that has not yet programmed a cassette combination), literally thousands of different specialized B cells are made in the bone marrow and are then "programmed" to each have only one option for antibody production.

CONNECTIONS

In this chapter, we have learned about the most important functioning molecule of the humoral immune system, the antibody or immunoglobulin. We have learned that there are five different types of immunoglobulins in the human body and each has its own purpose. We have also learned how antibodies bind to antigens and why the constant regions of the antibodies are important. Finally, we have learned the "trick" that our genes have played to give us thousands of different antibodies without having to have thousands of different genes to encode them. What we have not learned is how we trigger the B cells to make and secrete antibodies. We will explore this topic in our next chapter.

5

Making Antibodies

HOW AND WHEN ARE ANTIBODIES MADE?

Recall from the previous chapters that there are two classes of lymphocytes important in immunity. The B lymphocytes, or B cells, is the class most important for the humoral immune system. In addition, certain T lymphocytes and phagocytic cells are also important in antibody production. Recall that B cells are produced from bone marrow stem cells and that they remain in the bone marrow where they specialize and develop. During this development phase, the B cell becomes programmed to produce only one specific type of antibody. This antibody is unique and will only bind to one antigen. An antigen is a biological molecule that has a particular surface that is recognized by an antibody. This is a very specific binding, like a hand in a custom-made glove. Once the B cell specializes and matures, it coats its outer surface with IgD molecules that serve as antigen receptors or binding sites. These antigen receptors are critical for activation of the B cell and, therefore, for the production of antibodies.

Any large biological molecule can activate the immune system. These molecules are often proteins, but **polysaccharides**, complexes of sugars, and nucleic acids (DNA and RNA) can also serve to activate the humoral immune system. Viruses and microbial cells actually contain many different antigens on their surfaces, so it is possible to have more than one type of antibody that can bind to these cells. The first step in the humoral immune reaction is activation (Figure 5.1). Activation requires **antigens**, but the antigens have to

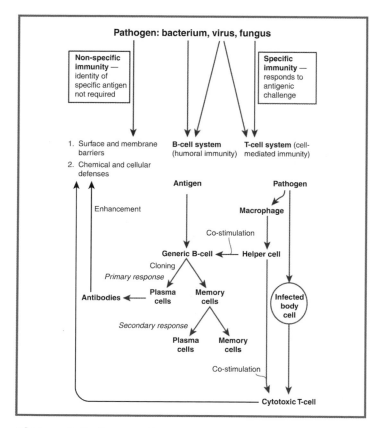

Figure 5.1 Many pathogens are excluded by the barriers of the skin and mucous membranes and the chemical defenses that constitute non-specific immunity. Should a pathogen breach these defenses, the actions of the humoral immune system (B-cell mediated) and the cell-mediated immune system (T-cell mediated) will attack the pathogen using very specific tools. Some pathogens are able to evade these two lines of defense and actually infect host cells. When this occurs, the infected cells will place antigens from the pathogen on their surfaces at the MHC I sites and cytotoxic T-cells specific to those antigens are recruited to destroy the infected cell. In other cases, the pathogens are engulfed by macrophages which present antigens from the pathogen on MHC II sites, recruiting T-helper cells. These T-helper cells can either stimulate the cell-mediated immune system via cytotoxic T cells or the humoral immune system by stimulated B cells (both the cytotoxic T cells and the B cells are antigen-specific). Finally, if a foreign antigen is present in the host, it will stimulate humoral immune response by recruiting generic B cells which undergo primary response, making both plasma cells and memory cells.

be attached to fairly big molecules. It is possible to have a biomolecule that is an antigen (an antigenic molecule) but which is too small to start the series of reactions needed for humoral response. Antigens that are big enough to start this process are called **immunogens**, which means "immune starting." Smaller antigens can be attached to another large complex molecule, and they too can become immunogenic. While there are lots of ways for the humoral immune system to activate, we will look at one example. We will explore what happens to the humoral immune system when it becomes exposed to a foreign bacterial cell. These same principles would apply for viruses and for other microorganisms.

A GERM INVADES: FIRST EXPOSURE ACTIVATION

Let us look at an example where a germ, a bacterium in this case, makes it past the innate immune system and enters the deeper tissues (see Figure 5.1 for an explanation of the different immune pathways). We will also assume that this is the first time this particular disease-causing bacterium has made it into the parts of your body that are protected by the acquired immune system. This might occur when you get cut on a dirty object or when your natural defenses are down and the bacterium makes it through the physical lines of defense. You will recall that there are phagocytic cells, macrophages that are part of the nonspecific immune system. They recognize that the bacterium is foreign to the body and they bind and engulf the bacterial cell.

Remember that once inside the macrophage, the enzymes and chemicals contained in vacuoles in the macrophage begin to attack the bacterium, breaking it down into little pieces. Once the bacterium is destroyed, the macrophage places the pieces of the bacterium, which contain antigens, on the macrophage cell surface at special sites called antigen-presenting sites.

As soon as these fragments of the bacterial cell are in place, the macrophage sends out chemical messages to attract a special group of lymphocytes called T helper cells. The T helper cells (T_H-cells) are attracted to the macrophage by these chemical messages. T_H-cells have special sites on their surface called CD4 receptors. These CD4 receptors bind very tightly to the antigen presenting site on the macrophage, but only if it is presenting an antigen. Once these T helper cells are bound to the macrophage, they are close enough to receive chemical messages from it. Leukocytes, both lymphoid cells like B cells and T cells, and non-lymphoid cells like macrophages, produce and release a host of different chemical messages called **interleukins**. Interleukin literally means "between leukocytes" and reflects the fact that these molecules transmit messages from one leukocyte to a different type of leukocyte. The messages change the behavior of the second cell. It can cause it to move toward the first cell as we saw for the first messenger molecule from the macrophage, or it can change the activity of the second cell in other ways. When the two cells are held together by binding of the CD4 receptor to the antigen-presenting site, a different interleukin is released from the macrophage that triggers the T-helper cell to produce and secrete its own interleukin messenger molecule.

The interleukin produced by the T-helper cell also serves as an attractant, but in this case, it recruits B lymphocytes (B cells) to the macrophage/T-helper complex. This interleukin attracts all B cells, regardless of the antibodies they produce. Most B cells will float into the area with the other two cells, but since they do not see an antigen on the macrophage antigen-presenting complex that they recognize, they will drift away. B cells that have IgD molecules on their surface that bind the antigen presented by the macrophage are attracted to the complex and bind to it. These B cells become tightly associated with the macrophage/T helper cell complex and remain at the site.

Once the B cell is in place, the T helper cell releases yet another interleukin. This interleukin molecule stimulates the B cell to reproduce. Why is this important? Remember that B cells are dedicated to only make a single antibody. Until exposed to an antigen, the body will only keep a very limited number of each B cell (probably less than 10) for any given antigen. We have assumed in this activation example that there was only one bacterial cell, but more likely, there will be hundreds or thousands of these bacterial cells. It will take more antibodies than ten B cells could produce to fight off the possible infection.

B CELL ACTIVATION

Once the B cell has been recruited to the complex by the interleukin released from the T helper cell, it is said to be "activated." The B cell will reproduce by mitosis (self-cloning), making many new B cells that produce the same antibodies. Because only B cells with IgD receptors that match the antigens

THE WORLD OF COCA-COLA®

Coca-Cola® is a worldwide corporation, and its signature drink, Coca-Cola®, has become an international business icon. Travel to almost any city in the world and you will find products from the Coca-Cola® Company. International headquarters for this multinational corporation is based in Atlanta, Georgia. If you are visiting downtown Atlanta, you might consider a visit to The World of Coca-Cola®, an interactive museum for the world's most popular soft drink. By far, the most popular stop on the tour is the tasting room. In addition to the company's very familiar drinks, Coca-Cola®, Sprite®, and Diet Coke®, the company makes dozens of other flavors. Some are very common around the world. Fanta®, the company's fruit flavored drinks, have some flavors, such as orange and grape, which are extremely popular and can be found in most parts of the world. Other flavors, tangerine, pineapple, and grapefruit, for instance, tend to be very popular in some cities, but not in others. These drinks are only needed in certain countries; consequently, the company produces them in only a limited number of their production facilities.

Perhaps one of the most regional flavors for Coca-Cola® is Beverly®. Beverly® is a bitters flavor drink. Interestingly, bitters are very popular drinks in Italy. The Coca-Cola® Company produces lots of Beverly at its facilities in Italy and virtually on the macrophage-presenting site are activated, all of the B cells that are produced by activation are programmed to make antibodies that will bind the presented antigen. This process is known as **B cell amplification** (Figure 5.2), which ensures that the body only amplifies B cells needed to attack the invading bacteria. As the B cells reproduce, they differentiate into two cell types. The first of these cell types is called a **plasma cell**. Plasma cells are very large cells that are dedicated factories for producing and secreting (releasing) antibody molecules. In our analogy to drink flavors (see box on page 62), the plasma cells

nowhere else. Some flavors of drinks change in popularity. Before the formulation of Diet Coke®, another diet drink made by Coca-Cola®, Tab®, was very popular and made in many of its plants. With the formulation of Diet Coke®, the popularity of Tab® has declined on a global scale. As a result, Coca-Cola® has reduced the number of plants that make Tab®, leaving it in production only where there is still a demand.

Our B cells can be viewed as different factories for different products. Just as the Coca-Cola® company makes different products on different manufacturing lines at different plants, our bodies make different antibodies from different B cells. As market demand for Coca-Cola® products increases, the number of plants making the product also increases, and as the demand decreases, plants are closed or redirected so they do not produce more of a flavor than the company can market. Our bodies regulate antibody production in much the same way. As the number of molecules of a particular antigen increases, the body will increase the number of B cells that make an antibody to attack that antigen. As the number of molecules of that antigen decreases, the number of B cells making the appropriate antibody also decrease. Our bodies monitor the "market" for particular antibodies and control production to meet the demand.

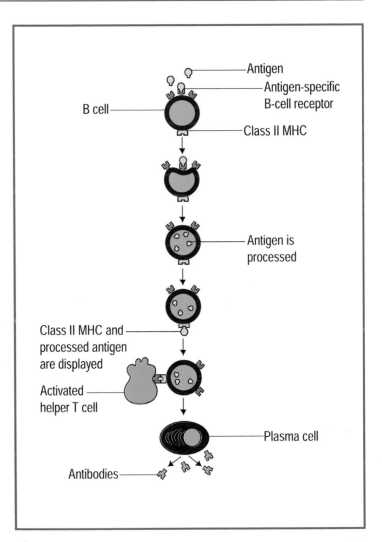

Figure 5.2 When a foreign antigen is present in the body, it binds to receptor sites specific for that antigen on B cells programmed to produce antibodies that bind that specific antigen. Once bound to the B cell surface, the antigen is internalized and processed. Portions of the antigen are presented on the surface of the B cell at MHC II sites. When these sites are occupied by the processed antigen they recruit T helper cells which release chemical signals that cause the B cell to become activated, making new plasma cells and memory B cells. The T helper cells, when stimulated by the presented antigen, also send out signals to recruit additional B-cells that can process the original antigen.

would be equivalent to the plants making a particular drink flavor. The other class of differentiated B cells is called **memory cells**. These cells are almost identical to the first B cell that was activated, and they do not produce and secrete antibodies. You might think of these as soft drink plants that are not producing a particular soda flavor, yet have all of the machinery and the formulations to do so. If the market demand goes up, that is, if at a later time the antigen is seen again, these cells can become quickly activated for production.

The plasma cells turn on their protein-making machinery. They make thousands of molecules of antibodies, each identical to the next. The antibody molecules are secreted into the plasma of the bloodstream or into the lymphatic fluid that bathes the tissues. As we learned in the last chapter, these antibodies are mostly IgM antibodies and, as a result, have multiple sites that can bind to antigens. Since viruses or bacterial cells have lots of antigens on their surfaces, the antibodies and antigen-covered cells form complexes. As these complexes form, the B cells release their own interleukins that attract phagocytic cells and complement proteins, eventually leading to the elimination of the bacterial cells.

The memory cells are functionally just like the original B cell, but there are many more of them for a given antigen than there were of the unamplified B cells. These remain in the body and can be activated if the body becomes exposed to the same bacterium in the future.

The process of activating these initial B cells, production of plasma cells and memory B cells, and the production of enough antibody molecules from the plasma cells to tie up all the bacterial cells and to allow the immune system to get rid of those cells takes about seven to ten days. Since the bacteria (or viruses) are reproducing all this time, they will often overwhelm the body and will result in disease symptoms. As we will see in the next section, future exposures allow the memory B cells to activate much more quickly, usually within two to four days. Since the body mounts the humoral response quickly, it tends to eliminate the microbes before they can cause enough damage to result in disease symptoms.

FIRST EXPOSURE USING VACCINES

It is possible to get the protection of an activated humoral immune system without suffering with a disease. In the last chapter we spoke of the MMR and the chickenpox vaccines and how these vaccines prevent many people from contracting these diseases. **Vaccines** are either made from microbes that are chemically altered so they cannot grow, are modified so they only cause very mild symptoms, or may consist of only one or two of the antigens, not the entire microbial cell. When we are vaccinated, the antigens that are introduced in the injection make the body think it has been infected by the microbe because the same antigens are present. These antigens will activate the immune system just as the infectious bacterium or virus will, but since the vaccine cannot cause disease, we get the benefit of B cell amplification and activation without becoming sick. Once the body has produced plasma cells and memory cells that respond to that antigen, the memory cells are already amplified and ready to respond if the microbe ever enters the body. The next section indicates what happens when the body is challenged by a microbe after an initial exposure.

ACTIVATION OF HUMORAL IMMUNITY—
SECONDARY RESPONSE

Once a B cell line has been activated and plasma and memory cells are generated from it, any future exposure to the same antigen (either the second exposure or the seventy-second one) is considered a "secondary" response. This is because every exposure after the first is just like every other subsequent exposure.

Once memory cells are in place for a specific antigen, the process of activation occurs just like it did for the first exposure if the body again experiences that antigen. If the antigen is on a bacterial cell, a macrophage will engulf and break down the cell into small pieces. These small bits of the cell, antigens, will be presented on the antigen-presenting sites on the surface of the macrophage. T helper cells are recruited which in turn will recruit memory B cells. When memory B cells enter the complex and bind to the antigen on the macrophage, these cells become activated and reproduce, making more plasma cells and additional memory B cells. Since there are so many more memory B cells for the antigen than there were inactivated B cells at the primary exposure, the memory B cells activate much more quickly, and large amounts of antibody are produced by the new plasma cells in less than half the time required for the first (primary) exposure.

However, the plasma cells made from memory B cells are reprogrammed to produce IgG antibodies rather than the IgM antibodies made by plasma cells made from the initial B cells. Huge amounts of antibody are released in the first few days, and the body destroys the microbe before it can cause the damage to the body that would result in symptoms of disease.

CONNECTIONS

In this chapter we have learned how the body amplifies the B cells it needs to respond to a particular antigen. We have learned how plasma cells make and secrete antibodies and how memory cells are stored, waiting for future exposures to the same microbe. We have also learned why a first exposure often results in disease, but future exposures do not, and how vaccines make it possible to avoid disease symptoms by making the body think it has seen a particular microbe before. Antibodies are very important in defending us from infection. However, there is another type of immunity, cell-mediated immunity, which functions very differently from humoral immunity, but is also important, especially in fighting some viral infections and certain rare types of cancer. The next chapter will discuss the importance of the cellular immune system and how it is controlled.

6

Cell-Mediated Immunity

T CELL TYPES

In the previous two chapters we have focused our attention on B lymphocytes, or B cells. T lymphocytes are closely related to B cells, however these cell precursors, generated from bone marrow stem cells, migrate to the thymus, a patch of fatty tissue located near the heart. In the thymus, T cells become programmed in a manner somewhat like B cell programming for B cells in bone marrow. T cells differentiate into three groups. T helper cells (T_H cells) we have already discussed. These are the cells that have CD4 receptors on their surfaces, allowing them to bind to macrophages and other phagocytic cells that are presenting foreign antigens. Recall that the T helper cell CD4 receptor binds to the antigen-presenting complex on the surface of a macrophage that has engulfed a foreign particle and which is presenting antigens from that substance at the antigen presenting site. This complex is called the Major Histocompatability Complex II (MHC-II). MHC-II is only found on the surface of phagocytic cells, thus only cells directly involved in removing foreign materials can bind the CD4 receptor on the T helper cell, and thereby, amplify the humoral immune response by recruiting and activating specific B cells.

All mammalian cells contain a second major histocompatability complex, MHC-I. These MHCs are unique for each species, and in fact, there can be different variants on MHC in different organisms of the same species (just as we can have different hair or eye color, blood type, etc.) These MHC-I proteins help us to recognize our own cells. If you are given a blood transfusion from a person with a different blood type, or if you receive transplanted organs from someone with a different MHC-I factor, the immune system will attack that organ, leading to rejection and major system failure in the body.

The second class of T cells, the cytotoxic T cells (T_C cells)

KILLERS FOR HIRE

Spy movies have become a staple for Hollywood. One of the more common elements in the spy movie formula is the hired assassin, or hired gun. These people learn everything they can about their targets so they kill the right person and not someone else by mistake. Typically, they are provided with detailed information so specific that the killer can distinguish their intended target from everyone else. A profile of a hired killer might include that they can specifically identify their target, that they go prepared with the necessary weapons to do the job, and once the job is finished, they fade back into obscurity so they cannot be identified.

The parts of the immune system involved in cell-mediated immunity are, in many ways, like hired killers. They are programmed to kill their targets without regret, and they are able to distinguish their target cells from all the other cells in the body. The immune cells carry powerful weapons with them to eliminate their targets, and once their job is done, they tend to disappear back into the blood stream so as not to bring attention to themselves.

Interestingly, the targets of the cell-mediated immune system are often our own cells. You might wonder about the logic of programming cells to destroy our own cells. The cell-mediated immune system usually only attacks our own cells when those cells present a danger to the rest of the body. Just as in spy movies where the target of hired killers are often traitors who threaten the safety and the security of the rest of society, our cell-mediated immune system has developed to identify our own cells that become cancerous and run the risk of creating tumors. The system also identifies cells which are infected with viruses and have become breeding grounds for those viruses, allowing for staging of a massive viral invasion of the host.

are very important in fighting viral and certain bacterial infections in our bodies, and they help to control certain rare forms of cancer. Cytotoxic T cells have CD8 receptors on their surfaces. These receptors bind to MHC-I on the surface of our own cells when those cells are presenting a foreign antigen. Why are the antigens on the surface of our cells? Viruses must infect specific host cells to reproduce. Many bacteria have developed mechanisms to penetrate into our cells as a way to "hide" from the humoral immune system. When a cell becomes infected by a virus or bacterium, it will present some of the antigens of that bacterium or virus on its surface at the MHC-I site.

If the infected cells are not removed they will burst, releasing lots of new viruses or bacteria. These organisms can then go on to infect more cells. For certain forms of cancer, cells that become carcinogenic (cancer-producing) make new proteins that are different from normal host proteins. These different proteins can also be presented on the cell surface. In the case of cancer cells, if they are allowed to grow without restriction, they will crowd out other cells, produce tumors, and lead to death. In short, infected human cells or cancer cells present a risk to the organism as a whole. They must be eliminated before they destroy the host.

When these cells present foreign antigens at the MHC-I site, cytotoxic T cells that are specialized for that antigen (just as B cells are programmed for a specific antigen, cytotoxic T cells are as well) respond. The CD8 receptor on the cytotoxic T cell binds to the MHC-I site and the IgD molecules on the surface of the cytotoxic T cell stabilize the complex by binding to the antigen. The T cells are then activated. T helper cells are also critical to the activation of cell-mediated immunity. They join the complex of the infected or cancerous cell and the cytotoxic T cell. An interleukin is produced that stimulates the T helper. The T helper cell, in turn, produces and secretes a different interleukin that activates the cytotoxic T cells in the complex. The first response of the T_C cell is to reproduce, just as we saw for activated B cells. When the number of cytotoxic T cells is high enough, they begin their attack.

T CELL RESPONSE AGAINST VIRUSES

When human cells are infected with a virus, they respond by breaking down certain cellular proteins that bind the virus and take its antigens to the MHC-I site on the surface (Figure 6.1). At this point, the infected cell is said to be "marked." The cytotoxic T cell uses the presented antigen and the CD8/MHC-I complex to bind to the surface of the infected cell. The T cell remains attached for about ten minutes. During this time, the T cell secretes a specialized class of proteins called **perforins**. The perforins penetrate into the membrane of the cell, associating with other perforins, ultimately producing a hole called a porin. These porins allow water to rush in from the outside of the cell, causing it to swell and eventually to burst. Thus, by killing the infected cell before the virus can finish replicating, the body breaks the chain reaction of viral infection, protecting the remaining cells of the body. This process will continue until all infected cells are killed.

A similar process eliminates certain forms of cancer cells. The cancer cells are determined to be foreign and are attacked by the cytotoxic T cells. Perforins are then used to puncture and lyse the cancer cell.

Finally, bacterial cells can infect host cells, especially macrophages. Some bacteria, including the species that causes tuberculosis, actually "trick" the macrophage into engulfing the bacterium. The bacterial cell is resistant to the action of the enzymes and chemicals in the macrophage and since the macrophage outer surface hides the antigens on the surface of the bacterium, these intracellular bacteria can continue to reproduce without threat from the humoral

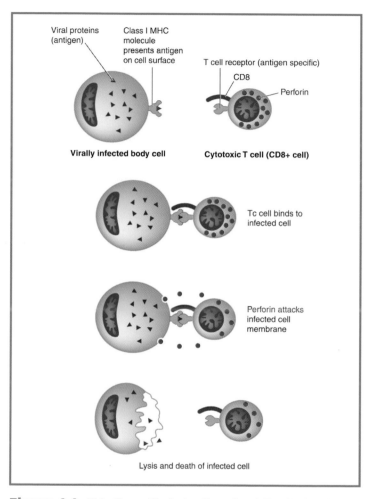

Viral proteins (antigen)

Class I MHC molecule presents antigen on cell surface

T cell receptor (antigen specific)

CD8

Perforin

Virally infected body cell

Cytotoxic T cell (CD8+ cell)

Tc cell binds to infected cell

Perforin attacks infected cell membrane

Lysis and death of infected cell

Figure 6.1 This figure illustrates the role of T cells in elimina-tion of infected host cells. If a host cell becomes infected with a virus, antigens from the virus are presented on the surface of the infected cell at MHC I complexes. The presence of an antigen at MHC I will recruit cytotoxic T cells that are programmed to specifi-cally recognize the presented antigen. The cytotoxic T cell binds to the infected cell through the CD8 receptor on its surface and the MHC I/antigen complex on the infected cell. Once the CD8 recep-tor binds, the cytotoxic T cell produces and secretes proteins called perforins. These proteins embed in the cell membrane of the infected host cells, creating holes in the membrane that ultimately cause the infected cell to rupture and die.

immune system. Macrophages actually contain both MHC-I and MHC-II complexes. Either or both can be used to present foreign antigens. Thus cytotoxic T cells will sometimes eliminate macrophages.

NON-B, NON-T CELLS

There is a third group of lymphocytes that are neither B cells nor T cells. Not surprisingly, these are called non-B, non-T lymphocytes. These cells are **natural killer (NK) cells**. They lyse human cells, much as cytotoxic T cells do, by producing and secreting perforins. These cells kill virus-infected host cells and certain cancer cells. They are also very important in rejection of transplanted tissues. The mechanism of recognition of these cells is unknown. The targeted cells must be presenting foreign antigens, but NK cells do not have receptors for specific antigens.

IMMUNE TOLERANCE

It would seem a risky proposition to have T cells that kill our own host cells. How are we sure that the immune system will not turn on us and attack our healthy cells? In some cases it does. These situations will be discussed in Chapter 8. Since the production of antibodies is a random assortment of cassettes in the antibody genes, why do we not make B cells and T cells that attack host tissue? Our immune system has an amazing ability to recognize its own or "self" antigens. This is called immune tolerance because the immune system usually does not attack these tissues. We do not fully understand this process, but we do know that as B cells and T cells activate in the bone marrow and thymus respectively, if their antigens are present (that is, a self antigen), the B or T cell that would respond to that antigen is destroyed through a process called apoptosis, or programmed cell death. In a healthy individual there will be lots of self antigens around and very few foreign antigens. As a result, immune tolerance destroys any lymphocyte that could attack a host tissue before it can amplify.

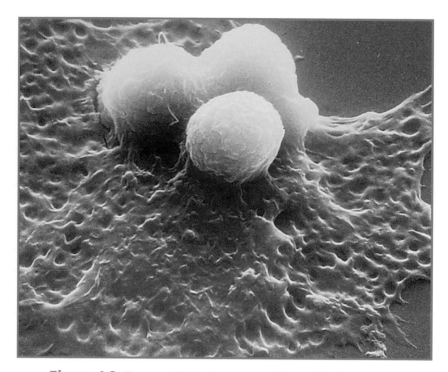

Figure 6.2 Tumor cells begin as normal host cells, but errors in regulation of cell replication cause them to become cancer cells. These tumor cells have unique surface antigens as compared with normal cells, and the cell-mediated immune system recognizes them as "foreign." When a macrophage detects these tumor cells with their foreign antigens, they first bind the cells to their surface, then activate the processes to engulf and chemically destroy the tumor cell, as can be seen in this electron micrograph of a macrophage surrounding three tumor cells (SEM, X 3,000).

CONNECTIONS

In this chapter we have seen that infected cells and cancer cells present a danger to the host organism (Figure 6.2). If unchecked, they will destroy many other cells and may lead to death. Cytotoxic T cells look for specific foreign antigens on the surface of infected host cells and produce perforins, which will punch holes in that cell, resulting in its destruction. By doing so, the cell is eliminated before the virus or bacterium can reproduce, or before the cancer cells can spread. By sacrificing a few cells, your cell mediated immune system protects the majority of others. We have also seen that there are some killer cells that do not look for a specific antigen, but somehow know when one of our cells has been compromised. These NK cells attack with perforins and destroy the dangerous cell before it can do more harm.

7

The Importance of Vaccines

WHAT IS IMMUNITY?

Immunity is a physical state of the body that makes it resistant to a particular disease. When you have immunity, you have B cells and antibodies and/or T cells that attack organisms that cause disease before the microbes have a chance to establish infection. There are actually four different kinds of immunity. These groups are divided by whether the immunity is a direct result of the action of the immune system (active) or from "borrowed" antibodies (passive). We can also characterize immunity based on whether it is acquired by a natural process or an artificial one.

Passive, artificial immunity occurs when we inject a person with antibodies from someone else. For instance, if someone in your family were to develop hepatitis, a liver disease caused by a virus, you and everyone else in your family might be advised to get "gamma globulin" shots. This involves receiving mixed serum from the blood of a number of different persons. If one of those people has previously been exposed to hepatitis, they will have antibodies in their serum against the virus. When the antibody is injected into you, you will be protected by the antibodies as long as they last, usually a few weeks. Another example of passive artificial immunity is used to treat poisonous snake bites. If you are bitten by a rattlesnake or copperhead (or any of a number of other snakes that make venom), the doctor may give you an injection of antitoxin. This is usually serum from an animal, a goat for instance, that has been exposed to the toxin. The goat antibodies will bind to the venom, isolating it and preventing it from damaging your tissues. The problem with this process is that goat antibodies are foreign to your body. You can take this treatment once, but your immune system will probably then make antibodies against the goat antibodies. If you are ever given goat serum again, you run the risk of a serious, even life-threatening reaction.

Passive, natural immunity is most commonly seen in infants. When a baby is first born, its immune system is not fully developed. It cannot make its own antibodies. Fortunately, while the baby is in the womb, antibodies from the serum of the mother enter the blood of the baby. Thus, the baby will have its mother's immunity for the first few weeks. This window of borrowed protection from the mother is further extended if the baby breast feeds. The mother will secrete IgA molecules in her breast milk, which enter the baby's body and protect her or him from disease.

Active, natural immunity occurs when you are exposed to an infectious organism for the first time. You will probably get sick, but for many diseases, your body turns on the immune system, providing protection against that same microbe in the future. Diseases like the major childhood diseases (measles, mumps, German measles, and chicken-pox) are all examples of diseases you typically will only have once.

Active, artificial immunity results from vaccination. We now vaccinate people against many of the more common human diseases. A vaccine is introduced into the body of a healthy person, usually by injection. The immune system reacts to the foreign vaccine and makes antibodies against it. When those antigens are seen again in the future, the immune system immediately responds, blocking the organism from causing disease. Vaccina virus, which causes cowpox, is a vaccine for smallpox. In this case a live virus is introduced below the skin of a healthy person. The virus causes a mild disease, but the antibodies the body produces as a result of this process protect against the much more serious smallpox virus. This is called a "live vaccine," but there are other types of vaccines.

THE DOCTOR, THE MILKMAID, AND THE BOY: A TRUE TALE

There are hundreds of human diseases, but none has been more devastating and feared than smallpox. However, you may have never heard of this disease. Although the disease was quite prevalent and responsible for millions of deaths prior to the later twentieth century, the disease no longer exists.

During the seventeenth century, smallpox was **epidemic** in Europe. Major outbreaks in some cases killed one-third of the population of many towns and cities. However, inhabitants of Asia and Africa had been using an ancient method of preventing the disease. This practice, called variolation (from the formal name for the smallpox virus, *Variola major*) involved placing scab material from a survivor of smallpox into a tiny cut in the skin of a healthy person. Usually the healthy person developed a mild form of the disease but recovered. Those who recovered from the disease seemed to be resistant to future outbreaks of smallpox. This method was introduced to Europe by Lady Montague, the wife of the British ambassador to Turkey.

In 1796, a country physician named Edward Jenner noticed that milkmaids seemed to be particularly resistant to smallpox. He soon discovered that all of these disease-resistant women had contracted a mild skin disorder that resulted in the formation of one or a few scabs, usually on the hands. He also discovered that the cows were subject to a skin disease called cowpox and that it was this disease, caused by a virus related

TYPES OF VACCINES

We have just seen the example of a live vaccine used to prevent smallpox. However, there are not always related viruses that we can use to protect against human illness. An alternative type of vaccine is made from an attenuated

to, but not identical to, the smallpox virus that the dairy maids had contracted.

Jenner hypothesized that if a person had a case of cowpox, he or she became resistant to smallpox. One of his patients, a young milkmaid named Sarah Nelms, agreed to allow Jenner to scrape some of the scab material from a cowpox wound on her hand. Jenner then used this material to inoculate (infect) 8-year-old James Phipps, another patient from the village who had never been exposed to smallpox (Figure 7.1). Other than feeling a bit sick, James had no other ill effects except for a blister at the site of the inoculation. Later, Jenner subjected James to variolation with scab material from a patient with smallpox. The boy did not become ill. Jenner repeated the variolation process on James. There was no sign of smallpox, not even a mild case. The cowpox exposure had made James resistant to smallpox.

Jenner called the treatment "vaccination." "Vacca" is the Latin word for "cow." Very quickly, Edward Jenner's vaccination procedure became standard treatment to prevent smallpox. Because the cowpox virus and the smallpox virus are closely related, immunity to cowpox also provides protection against smallpox. The procedure remained the preferred way to protect from smallpox for over three hundred years. A few patients would have severe reactions to cowpox vaccination, and a very low number would die, but the risk was much lower of dying from vaccination than from a natural case of smallpox.

Figure 7.1 Edward Jenner, an English physician, is credited with discovering the first effective vaccine. By taking a small amount of the wound material from a cowpox pustule and introducing it into a healthy individual through a number of scratches on the skin, Jenner created a cowpox infection (*Vaccinia*) at the inoculation site. Once recovered from this mild, local infection, the person immunized was resistant to smallpox. The term "vaccine" which we use for any artificial method to induce the immune system is derived from the Latin word "vaccinus," which means "of the cow." In this painting, Jenner is vaccinating his first patient, James Phipps.

microorganism. An attenuated microorganism has been transferred through a series of individual animals that are not good hosts for that microbe. Over time, the virus becomes weakened, or attenuated. You can then use the attenuated virus to vaccinate other organisms. This has been used effectively for a number of diseases, including rabies. Unfortunately, sometimes attenuated organisms will mutate back to forms that cause serious disease. For that reason, attenuated vaccines must be carefully monitored.

One can also make a vaccine by chemically altering a microorganism so it can no longer cause disease, but so that it retains enough of its antigens that it can immunize you against future cases of the disease. Treating bacteria or viruses with formaldehyde is a common way to alter the organism so that it no longer reproduces; yet it retains enough of its original nature to turn on the immune system.

Finally, in the past few years scientists have developed vaccines from only parts of a microorganism. This can be done by cloning the gene for an important surface protein for the bacterium or virus and injecting just that one protein into the patient. If antibodies are made to the protein, those antibodies will protect you from the intact organism. We have also developed ways to use DNA and other components of the microbial cell to make vaccines.

HOW ARE VACCINES ADMINISTERED?

Vaccines have been traditionally administered through injection. In some cases, the vaccine is injected just below the skin (subcutaneously) and in other cases, it is injected into muscle (intramuscularly). Both methods allow for the antigen or antigens in the vaccine to diffuse into the bloodstream slowly, allowing a continuous activation of the immune system over several days. In order to amplify the number of B and T cells that respond to the vaccine,

(continued on page 84)

SMALLPOX AND THE FUTURE

Around the middle of the twentieth century, scientists and physicians determined that since smallpox (Figure 7.2) could only infect humans, if a massive vaccination effort could be orchestrated globally, it might be possible to eradicate the virus that causes smallpox. The World Health Organization, the public health authority for the United Nations, took up the smallpox challenge and by the mid-1970s, the last natural case of smallpox was recorded. The medical community had done something that had never before been accomplished. They had completely eliminated a human disease. This was accomplished through a massive vaccination program, focusing on all the people that lived in the area immediately around smallpox outbreaks. It was hard work, but they succeeded. Smallpox was no more, and since there was now a higher risk of dying from vaccination than from being exposed to smallpox, the vaccination program was terminated. You may know someone who received a smallpox vaccination. Usually they will have a scar on the upper left arm, the site where cowpox was introduced into the body with several shallow point needles.

The elimination of smallpox was a modern miracle. The world scientific community discussed destroying all stocks of the smallpox virus, but decided that two stocks would be maintained should there ever be another smallpox outbreak. One stock was maintained in the United States, at the Centers for Disease Control and Prevention (CDC) in Atlanta, Georgia. The other was maintained in a laboratory in Russia. Since the fall of the Soviet Union, there are now concerns that the Russian smallpox stock may have been compromised and the virus could be in the hands of persons who would use it as a weapon or as a tool of terror. The risk of smallpox has returned, and the government of the United States is now determining how to reinstate a vaccination program. Those scars on the left arm may soon reappear as a testament to our failure to protect the world from this killer virus.

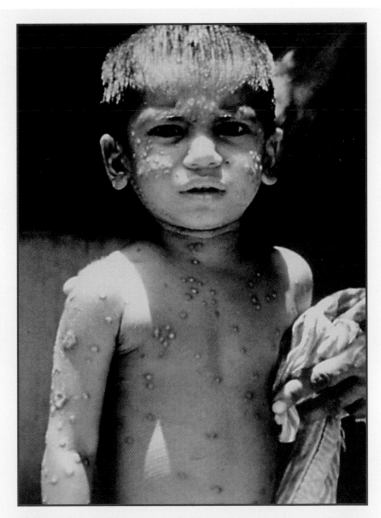

Figure 7.2 Smallpox was once one of the most feared diseases of humanity. About one in three people who contracted the disease died, and those that survived were permanently scarred from the pustules that formed when the virus infected the host. The young boy in this picture is suffering from smallpox. Although smallpox has been eliminated from the earth, stocks of the virus were maintained for research purposes. Some officials feel that if the stocks fall into the wrong hands, the disease could be used as a biological weapon.

(continued from page 81)

multiple vaccinations may be required over weeks or months. In all cases where vaccines are injected, the majority of the antibody raised is in the bloodstream, usually in the form of IgG, although low levels of antibody can be found on the mucous membranes (usually IgA) and in other locations throughout the body (the specific immunoglobulin type at these other locations varies).

In recent years, the notion of localized immunization has gained popularity. This is particularly promising for vaccination against disease. Most microbes have specific sites where they enter the body. Those pathogenic microbes that cause infections of the mouth, nose, throat, and lungs (respiratory pathogens) usually gain entry to the body by crossing the mucous membranes. New vaccines have been developed which are given as a nasal spray. These have proven as effective as injections in raising levels of antibody in the blood, but more importantly, inhaled vaccines raise a very active immune response at the mucous membranes themselves. This ensures that the antibodies bind the microbes just as they are entering the body, thus reducing the degree of damage that results to the tissues. There are also efforts to develop ingested vaccines to protect from diseases of the intestinal tract. Applying the vaccine through the same portal of entry as the microbes the vaccines are designed to fight speeds up the response time of the immune system and its efficiency.

CONNECTIONS

In this chapter, we have learned that there are a number of ways to acquire antibodies. We can produce them in our own bodies by natural means of exposure to antigens or through the use of vaccines. We can also get antibodies from others, either as injected serum or, in the case of an infant, from the mother either before birth or through breast milk. Vaccines can be live microbes, weakened microbes, inactivated microbes, or parts of microbes. Finally, while most vaccines are currently given by injection, new methods of delivering vaccines to the site where the microbe enters the body may be very effective in preventing disease.

8

Allergies and Autoimmune Diseases — Defense Becomes Offense

ALLERGIC REACTIONS

One of the most common problems that results from a functional immune system is an allergic reaction. Allergic reactions result when the body comes in contact with an antigen, thus activating the immune reaction, which results in a severe inflammatory response. Recall that when we discussed the antibodies, or immunoglobulins, we mentioned that one class of these, the IgE class, was particularly involved in allergic reactions. IgE molecules look very much like IgG except they have a different constant region. The constant region of the IgE molecule binds receptor sites on mast cells and granulated white blood cells. In the absence of an antigen attached at the variable region of IgE, the immunoglobulin does not bind these cells, but when antigens are bound at the variable regions (the arms of the "Y"), the proteins making up the immunoglobulin shift, exposing the site that binds mast cells and granular leukocytes. When the antibody molecules bind to these cells, the cells release their granules, including histamine, a very powerful inflammatory mediator.

When histamine is released, the molecule immediately initiates the inflammatory response. The capillaries become leaky, and fluid leaks into the tissues around the antigen/antibody complex. This causes swelling, reddening, and heat. Additionally, the increased fluid stimulates nerve cells in the area, causing a

CONFIDENCE AND CAMPING: A TRUE STORY

As a teenager I worked one summer at a Boy Scout camp in north Georgia. One of my duties was to teach the requirements for Second Class and First Class scouts. One of the topics required at that time was plant identification, particularly those plants that were poisonous and should be avoided when camping. While following one of the nature trails, I pointed out to my class the three-leafed poison ivy and poison oak plants. I explained how these plants contain an oil that causes allergic reactions in many people. One particularly arrogant scout announced to everyone that he was not allergic to poison ivy, and before I could stop him, he grabbed a handful of leaves, rubbed them all over his body, then put them in his mouth, chewed and swallowed!

The next morning the young man was a sight to see. His face was so swollen that he could not open his eyes. A red rash covered his body and because he had swallowed leaves, his throat was swollen to the point where he was having difficulty breathing. He had to be rushed to the local hospital, admitted, and intubated so he could breathe. He then began a series of painful injections of cortisones, compounds that short circuit the immune system, in an effort to reduce the reaction.

This young man learned an important lesson. Just because you do not display an allergic reaction the first time you are exposed to an antigen does not mean you never will. The oil in poison ivy and poison oak plants is a huge molecule, with hundreds of different antigens. A first, second, or even third exposure, if minor, might not have caused an allergic reaction, but each time you are exposed to one of these multi-antigenic molecules, you run the risk of activating an immune reaction. In this case, the immune reaction does not help the body; it harms it and, in some cases, can be fatal.

severe itching sensation. In some cases, such as a skin rash, the inflammatory condition may not be life-threatening, but it can be uncomfortable. In other cases, it can cause damage to certain organs. In a few cases of allergic reaction, the inflammatory response can be so severe and so much fluid can leak from the circulatory system that the blood pressure drops and the body can enter a life-threatening condition. Most often these life threatening reactions, called **anaphylactic reactions** (Figure 8.1), occur when the antigen is introduced into the blood or deeper tissues. This condition requires immediate intervention. Anaphylactic reactions can occur to foods, drugs, or even bee stings. If a person is allergic to certain foods he or she must avoid them or run the risk of dying from the allergic reaction. In cases of bee stings, one cannot always avoid exposure to bee venom. Most people with severe reactions to bees will carry a syringe with epinephrine. When injected, epinephrine causes an immediate block of the inflammatory response. In still other cases of allergies, you may be able to minimize symptoms by taking antihistamines. These drugs block the action of histamine, thus preventing the inflammatory response. In some cases, cortisones are given which short circuit the immune system, reducing inflammation and all its symptoms.

HAY FEVER

A very common form of allergic reaction is hay fever. If you have allergies to dust, dust mites, molds, or pollens, you can inhale them when they are in the air. Once in the respiratory tract, these allergens stimulate an inflammatory response. This leads to swelling of the tissues of the nose, throat, and lungs. As the tissues swell with fluid they close off the airway, making it hard to breathe and causing the symptoms of a "stuffy nose." The release of fluids may also cause your nose to run and your eyes to tear, and the inflammation in the area will often cause the nose and eyes to turn red. If you have a relatively mild case

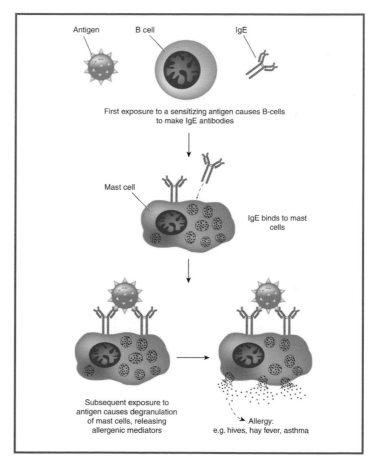

Figure 8.1 Anaphylaxis is a serious allergic response that can occur when a person is exposed to foreign antigens such as those found in some foods, venoms, and medications (recall that not all persons are allergic to these things). When a person allergic to these antigens is first exposed, special B cells produce a class of antibodies called IgE antibodies. These antibodies are structurally like IgG, but have a different constant region. The constant region of the IgE molecule with bound antigen will then bind to receptors on a special group of cells, called mast cells. The next time the foreign antigen is experienced by the host, the IgE molecules will bind to the variable regions (the "arms"). This stimulates the attached mast cell to degranulate (release its stores of allergic mediators such as histamine). These mediators cause inflammatory responses. An example of anaphylactic hypersensitivity is diagrammed here.

of hay fever you probably manage it with nose sprays and anti-histamines. If the case is more serious, you may require an inhaler to reduce the swelling of the tissues around the airway allowing you to breathe more easily. In some cases, the allergic reactions are so bad, your doctor may send you to an allergist for allergy shots.

What exactly are allergy shots and how do they work? One of the first things the allergist will do is to determine exactly which allergens are the problem. She or he will do this by taking samples of the most common allergens, plant pollens, molds, dust mites, and a variety of other agents, and then will place a small amount of this material under the skin at a spot that has been labeled with the code for that particular antigen (Figure 8.2). A standard allergy screen will usually involve fifty or so different allergens, a negative control (usually water) and a positive control (histamine). These allergens are introduced with pins dipped in the allergen, then pricked into the skin. You will get most of these specimens placed on your back, with some on your arms as well. If a particular spot turns red, swollen, and itchy within 24-48 hours, this indicates that you are allergic to that allergen.

Once the allergist knows what allergens cause the problem, he or she will order a special mixture of these allergens at very low concentrations. Allergy shots are mixes of the allergens to which you are allergic. It sounds crazy. Doctors are injecting the things you are allergic to under your skin, but this is done repeatedly and with increasing amounts of the allergen. After a while, your body begins to think the allergen is a normal "self" protein. Your **T Suppressor** cells, the last class of T cells, will target the cytotoxic T cells that bind that antigen, and more importantly, the B cells that produce antibodies against the allergen. Eventually, if all works well, you will destroy those T and B cell lines that cause the allergic reaction. Once this process is complete, you will no longer suffer allergic reactions to that antigen. Your allergic reactions lessen, and you find that

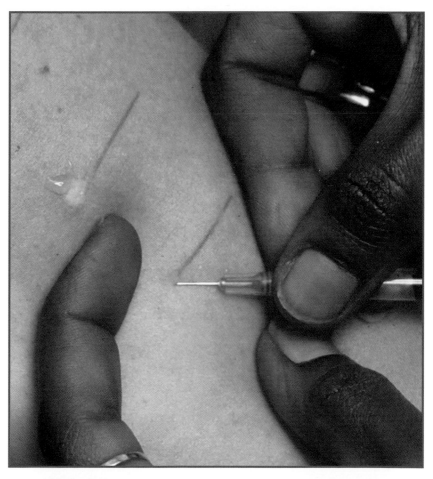

Figure 8.2 When people are suspected of having allergies they usually go to a medical specialist, an allergist, to determine the source of the allergy and the appropriate treatment. Allergy testing involves introducing a small amount of a suspected allergen under the skin. If the patient is allergic to the allergen, a localized inflammatory response occurs at the site of injection, causing the area to become red, swollen, and to itch. Allergists will usually use a "panel" of two dozen or more of the most common allergens to test the patient. This will usually be administered by creating a grid on the back and arms with markers and testing a different allergen in each area. These allergens are introduced by pricking the skin with a small pin or needle that has a small amount of the allergen (which is an antigen) on its tip, as is shown in this photograph.

you can tolerate your hay fever or other allergic reaction better as a result.

AUTOIMMUNE DISEASES

Recall that the body normally eliminates the T cells and B cells that can react with normal "self" proteins. Our bodies do this, probably in fetal development and early childhood, and as a result we do not have our immune system attacking our own tissues. Unfortunately, in some cases our bodies fail to eliminate the B and T cells that recognize our own antigens. These lead to some very serious diseases collectively known as autoimmune diseases. In the following sections we will look at some of the more common autoimmune diseases.

Juvenile Diabetes

You may have friends who have diabetes and have had this ailment since they were small children. Chances are that these friends have juvenile diabetes, also called insulin-dependent, or Type I diabetes. Most diabetics that suffer from this disease develop it between the ages of four and six. We know there is a genetic basis for the disease because children of parents with juvenile diabetes have a much higher risk of the disease than children of parents who do not have the disease. Diabetes is a condition where the body either stops producing insulin (Type I) or stops responding to insulin (Type II). Insulin is a hormone that controls the level of glucose in the blood. If glucose levels get too high, the body secretes insulin, which is made in the pancreas, into the blood stream where it stimulates muscle cells to take up and burn glucose. This restores the glucose to normal levels. If your body does not get rid of excess glucose, you will become tired, you will not think clearly, and you may become grouchy. Since persons with juvenile diabetes do not make insulin they must take injections of insulin, often multiple times a day. They must carefully monitor what they eat and how much exercise they perform in order to balance the amount of insulin they give themselves. If they give too little, the glucose levels will get too high and this can result in damage to the circulatory system, the eyes, and the kidneys. If they give too much, the glucose levels will drop to dangerously low levels, which can put them into shock. As you can see, diabetes is a serious disease that requires careful management, but what does it have to do with the immune system?

People with juvenile diabetes do not have a gene that will allow them to destroy B cells that make antibodies against the islet cells of the pancreas. As a result, the body makes antibodies and cytotoxic T cells that attack these cells, which are the cells that produce insulin. Juvenile diabetes is an autoimmune disease because the body's immune system destroys the cells that make insulin.

Rheumatoid Arthritis

Have you ever met anyone with rheumatoid arthritis? If so, the chances are you have noticed that the joints, particularly those of the fingers and hands, are swollen and may be disfigured (Figure 8.3). Rheumatoid arthritis is another autoimmune disease. The skeletal system contains soft tissues on the ends of the bones that serve as cushions. This prevents the bones from grinding against one another when you move. In the case of rheumatoid arthritis, the body makes antibodies that attack these soft tissues. This causes a massive inflammatory reaction at the site of the joints. The constant swelling due to inflammation causes joint pain, the formation of swollen knots at the joints, and eventually causes damage to the bones themselves, resulting in disfigurement. Like most disabling autoimmune diseases, the only way to treat this condition is to short circuit the immune system. This reduces the pain and damage from inflammation, but it

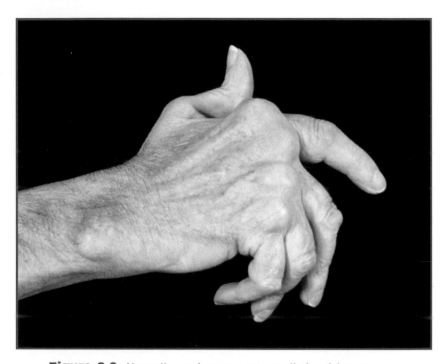

Figure 8.3 Normally our immune system distinguishes our own antigens as "self" and foreign antigens as "non-self." Our bodies are programmed not to attack self antigens. In some cases, however, the immune system will fail to recognize some of our antigens as "self" and will attack our own tissues. The diseases that result are called autoimmune diseases. Rheumatoid arthritis is an example of an autoimmune disease. In this case, the immune system attacks the soft tissues that line and cushion the joints. The chronic inflammation that results will cause the joints to swell and can result in deformation of the joints and accumulation of scar tissue. This figure illustrates the damage done to the hand of an elderly patient who has suffered from rheumatoid arthritis for many years.

makes the patient more susceptible to infection. As a result, patients under treatment for rheumatoid arthritis tend to get sick more often than people who do not have to suppress their immune systems. If left untreated, the inflammation at the joints may completely destroy the joints and bones, which can lead to permanent disability.

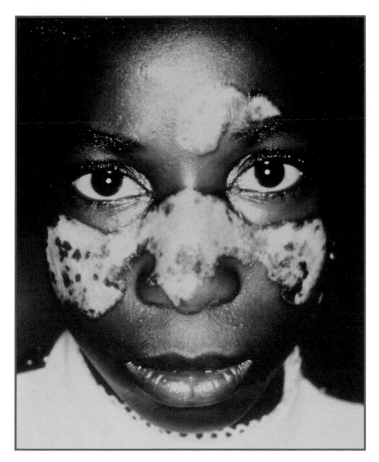

Figure 8.4 Lupus is another example of an autoimmune disease. In this case, the body's immune system attacks the connective tissue of the skin. This figure illustrates a "butterfly rash" on the face of a Lupus patient. This rash does not always occur in lupus cases, but seldom occurs in non-lupus patients. Lupus can be life-threatening as the immune system can attack the connective issue of major organs of the body, resulting in failure of essential body functions.

Lupus

The last example of an autoimmune disease we will discuss is lupus, often called systemic lupus, because it affects the entire body. Lupus is an autoimmune disease where antibodies and

T cells target the connective tissue of the skin and internal organs. This causes damage to the skin and is often characterized by unusual rashes with no apparent cause (Figure 8.4). As the antibodies attack the connective tissue, not only is the skin affected, but so too is the connective tissue of the inner organs. If untreated, this can lead to failure of one or more of the essential organs, resulting in death. Lupus is a progressive disease for which there is no cure. Management of lupus involves suppression of the immune system. As in the case of rheumatoid arthritis patients, lupus patients receiving immunosuppression therapy must be very careful to avoid infections, as they are less able to fight off microbes.

ARTIFICIAL AUTOIMMUNE RESPONSES
Blood Transfusions

Persons who do not have autoimmune diseases can consider themselves fortunate. Ironically, in some cases, medical practices may subject patients to autoimmune-like reactions. These occur in cases where there are errors in blood transfusions or organ transplants.

Human blood consists of four major blood types. Types A and B each contain one type of antigen on the surface of the red blood cell. If a person has Type A blood they do not make antibodies against the A antigen because it is a "self" antigen; however, there is nothing to prevent them from making anti-Type B antibodies (antibodies that bind B antigens). Likewise, a person with Type B blood will have B antigens on the red blood cells and will not have anti-Type B antibodies in the serum, but could make anti-Type A antibodies. The third blood type, AB, has red blood cells with both A and B antigens on the red blood cells. People with Type AB blood will not produce either anti-A or anti-B antibodies. This means they can receive any blood (A, B, AB, or O) and the will not reject the blood. For this reason, persons with AB blood are called universal recipients because they can accept any of the major blood types. The fourth group of blood types is Type O. People with Type O have neither A or B antigens on their red blood cells. They can produce both anti-A and anti-B antibodies and as a result, they can only accept Type O blood, however, they can donate red blood cells to anyone because there are neither A or B antigens on the cells to react with antibodies. This is why Type O persons are called "universal donors." Of course, the A, B, O antigen system is not the only group of antigens in blood. Consequently, not every Type A patient can take blood from every other Type A patient. The other antigens must match as well, but we will not explore these other antigen systems on blood as it is beyond the scope of this book.

If a patient receives blood from a donor who does not match for the major antigens, they may have very little reaction the first time (depending on how much blood they are given). The new blood cells have antigens that are foreign. These will induce select B cells to secrete antibodies that will bind these cells. It may be that these blood cells are "turned over," or dissolve before the antibodies can be produced. However, if the same patient is ever exposed to that foreign blood type again, he or she will activate a rapid response. Antibodies form clumps with the foreign blood cells (Figures 8.5a and 8.5b). This reduces the ability of the blood to transport oxygen, but perhaps more seriously, it can lead to blockage of the capillaries that supply blood and therefore oxygen to the vital organs. Damage to the vital organs can result and death is not unusual. This is why doctors require that labs "type and cross match" any blood they give to a patient against a sample of the patients own blood.

These tests will allow the lab technician or technologist to detect clumping if the bloods do not match, and a different unit of blood can be tested. In the case of emergencies where there is no time to type and cross match blood, a doctor may give the patient saline (to raise the volume of

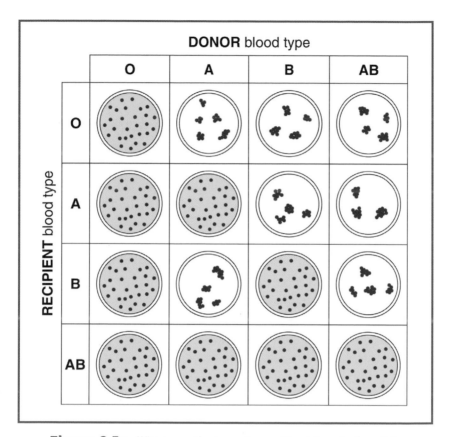

Figure 8.5a When a patient requires a blood transfusion, it is essential that the patient's blood and the unit of blood to be given be typed and crossmatched. This test is done by taking a small amount of the patent's blood and mixing it with the available units of blood in the blood bank. In the figure above, samples of each of the major blood groups are mixed with each other. Note that when blood of the same major blood group are mixed (O with O, A with A, etc.), the red blood cells stay evenly distributed. Others, when mixed, will create clumps of antibody and red blood cells, as can be seen when Donor type A is mixed with Recipient Type O.

fluid in the blood stream, or possibly will give units of O negative blood which is least likely to cross react with serum in a patient's blood (the "negative" refers to the Rh factor, a separate antigen).

Figure 8.5b By testing for the presence of red blood cell antibodies, A and B, you can determine the major blood type of any patient. A positive reaction occurs when antibodies in the reagent attach to antigens on the surface of the red blood cells. This causes the red blood cells to clump as the antibodies bridge between cells, making many cells stick together (top well). If only the A antiserum (the reagent made from serum containing antibodies against the antigen, in this case the A blood group antigen) reacts, the patient has Type A blood. If only the B antiserum reacts, the patient has Type B blood. If both react, the patient has Type AB blood. If neither type of antiserum reacts with the blood sample, the blood is Type O (Type O means "null", or neither A or B antigens are on the red blood cells).

Unfortunately, not enough people donate blood. Sometimes the supply of blood becomes so low that surgeons have to cancel elective surgeries, and emergency patients have been known to die because not enough of the right blood type was available. For this reason, scientists are looking at new ways to meet the blood demand. Some are trying to develop artificial blood; this would not contain blood cells, but would have other chemicals that could transport oxygen and carbon dioxide. If artificial blood could be developed, it could save many lives, but we have not succeeded in this effort so far. A more promising approach is blood type conversion. We now know there are enzymes that can remove the A and B antigens from red blood cells. Treating blood with these enzymes would result in essentially all blood being Type O. If we can find a way to remove all of the antigens from the surface of red blood cells without destroying the function of the cells, we could make blood typing obsolete. We would still need blood donors, but at least all units of blood could be given to all patients. Research continues in this area.

Organ Transplant Rejection

The last example of a case where the immune system may harm more than help is in the area of organ transplants. Recall that all cells in the body have the same MHC-I complexes on their surfaces. Different people can have different MHC complexes. Since all of the cells, and therefore all of the organs are tagged with these MHC complexes, before a patient can receive an organ transplant doctors have to match the donor and recipient MHC antigens as best they can. If you receive an organ from someone with a different MHC complex, your body will assume the organ is foreign and will begin attacking it. This is what happens when a transplant patient "rejects" an organ. As much of a problem as blood donations can be, organ donations are an even bigger problem. Not nearly enough people donate their organs when they die. As a result, there are always many more people who need an organ than there are matching organs. Thousands of people die in this country every year because they cannot get matching organs when they need them. Since MHC complexes are genetically coded, persons of one race are more likely to have the same blood type and organ type as others in their race than people of different races.

Finding matching organs is particularly difficult for Hispanic or African-American patients because people in these groups have traditions that make organ donation less likely. It is important to remember that in most cases (with the possible exception of kidney transplants and cornea transplants) organs are harvested from people who have recently died.

CONNECTIONS

As you have learned in this chapter, while our immune system is very important in avoiding and fighting infection, it can also be the source of health problems. We can have allergic reactions to pollen in the air, resulting in hay fever, or to certain foods or beverages which can cause problems ranging from a mild rash, to vomiting and nausea, to more life threatening reactions. In some cases, we are allergic to proteins in things such a bee venom where even a single bee sting may cause us to experience a life-threatening condition called anaphylaxis.

The immune system is also the source of most of our problems faced with blood transfusions and organ transplants. If blood and organs are not carefully matched to the blood or tissues of the person receiving the transfusion or transplantation, the results can be deadly. Finally, in some cases our immune system fails to recognize our own tissues and may produce antibodies that attack part of our own body. This can lead to long-term debilitating illnesses or in some cases, death.

The immune system is extremely powerful. It must be to

ORGAN TRANSPLANTS

The immune system plays a critical role in organ transplants. The MHC antigens on the donor's organs must match those present in the recipient or the recipient's body will attack the new organs. Even with a nearly perfect match, there is still a chance or rejection.

Recently, the delicacy of organ transplantation made national headlines when a young girl received a mismatched heart-lung transplant. She had spent three years on the donor waiting list as a result of a heart deformity that prevented her lungs from depositing oxygen in her blood.

However, what seemed like a routine transplant needed to save this girl's life became a complicated test of scientific know-how. When the Donor Services contacted the doctor in charge, they had another potential recipient in mind for the available organs. Because the first patient was not ready for transplant, the doctor inquired as to whether the heart and lungs might be available for the young girl. Unfortunately, Donor Services and the doctor never discussed blood-type compatibility. Donor and recipient matching is divided into three main areas: blood type matching, tissue matching, and cross matching. Each qualification refers to both the donor and recipient's condition. These tests used to determine a match are used to rate the overall expected success for the transplant.

In this young girl's case, the qualifications were overlooked, setting up an even more complicated situation for the young girl. Unfortunately, due to human error, organs that had type A blood, which did not match her type O-positive blood, replaced her heart and lungs. Because of the mismatch, her body initially rejected the transplant. Soon after the surgery, the surgical team received a call from the hospital's Transplant fight infection, but when the normal checks and balances of the immune system are ignored or overridden by the body, the immune system may become our worst enemy rather than our close ally.

Immunology Laboratory reporting the organs were incompatible with the girl's blood type. Doctors began the incitation of plasmapheresis (separation of blood plasma components to remove immune-active components) and high dose immuno-suppressants, drugs that shut down the immune system in order to prevent organ rejection. The hospital immediately contacted United Network for Organ Sharing about the ABO incompatibility and the girl's need for new organs.

Because of the severity of her situation, the young girl's name went to the top of the donor list. Within two weeks of her first operation, which was unusually fast despite her priority status, a second set of organs was located. Soon thereafter the girl underwent her second heart-lung transplant. Doctors claimed that the organs were working perfectly after the second surgery and were hopeful about her chances. How-ever, too much damage had been done to her body for her to recover. She had been near death by the time she underwent her second surgery. The treatment she received to prevent her body from rejecting the organs was necessary, but the length of time had greatly weakened her body. Following the second transplant, she experienced bleeding and swelling in her brain. Further tests reveled that that there was no electrical brain activity and no blood flow to the brain. Shortly there-after, the girl was removed from life support. Although the hospital has since changed its policies regarding transplant surgeries (now three members of the transplant team are required to confirm the compatibility of the donated organs with the organ recipient), controversy is still swirling around the tragedy of this girl's death. Hopefully, one tragedy can prevent the same accident from occurring again.

9

Immunity as a Tool for Scientists

DIAGNOSTIC IMMUNOLOGY

Our understanding of immunology has changed dramatically over the past thirty years. What was poorly understood in the 1980s has become one of the fastest growing and most significant areas of science. It has also become one of the most practical areas. Immunological processes are among the most common and most important diagnostic tests used in the laboratory. Remember that antibodies (immunoglobulins) are extremely specific. A given antibody will only bind to a single antigen, or perhaps a group of very closely related antigens. This high degree of specificity makes antibodies a powerful tool for detecting specific proteins, polysaccharides, and other large molecules. This specificity has allowed us to develop antibody-based reagents (supplies used in the laboratory) to detect specific molecules. We will explore some of the more common applications of antibodies for diagnostic tests.

PRECIPITATION REACTIONS

One of the first tests to be developed was the precipitation test. The basis of this test is simple. Every antibody molecule has two or more antigen binding sites. These sites bind identical antigens. Cells, whether they are blood cells or bacterial cells, tend to have many copies of the same antigens on their cell surfaces. If you mix a suspension of these cells with serum containing an antibody for one of the surface antigens of the cell, the antibodies will begin binding

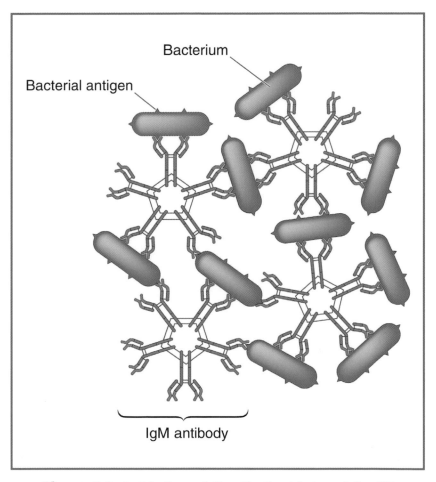

Figure 9.1 In this figure, IgM antibodies (clusters of five "Y" antibody subunits) are added with antigens that bind at the variable regions. Note that all ten variable regions of the IgM antibody (two regions per "Y") bind the same antigen. The IgM antibody in this case binds a surface antigen on a bacterial cell. There are usually many copies of this antigen per cell. As a result, large complexes of antibody and antigen are formed. These large complexes of bacterial cells and antibodies are easily recognized by the immune system, allowing the body to eliminate invading bacteria quickly.

to different cells, and since the cells have lots of antigen sites, they will bind multiple copies of antibodies. Very quickly, the cells will clump together and will form such large complexes that they will fall out of solution, or precipitate (Figure 9.1).

A practical example of the precipitation test is blood grouping. If you take a sample of blood from a person who is Type B and you mix a drop of that blood with serum containing anti-B antibodies, the blood cells will clump together. This will cause the normally even suspension of blood cells to become very "grainy" in appearance. The formation of grains of cells indicates that the blood cells contain the B antigen. If you were to mix a drop of the same blood sample with serum containing anti-Type A antibodies, these antibodies would not bind the antigens on the blood cells, and the blood cells would remain evenly spread throughout the suspension. Blood from a person with the AB blood type would precipitate in both samples of serum, and Type O blood, which has neither A nor B antigens on its red blood cells, would not clump in either serum. With just two serum samples, one that binds A antigen and one that binds B antigen, we can distinguish the four major blood groups.

Another common precipitation test is the double diffusion test. This test involves small wells which are punched into a gelled matrix. If you put serum against a particular antigen in the center well and you put protein (antigen) samples in several surrounding wells you can determine how related those protein samples are to one another. The antibodies in the serum will begin to diffuse into the gel and will move outward. The proteins in the surrounding wells will diffuse through the gel toward the center well. When the antibody and an antigen that binds to it diffuse to the same place, the proteins precipitate. This creates a visible, milky-colored band between the wells. You will only get these lines of precipitation if the antigen in a well is bound by the antibody in the serum. If these two proteins don't bind together, they continue to diffuse and will not precipitate.

Scientists have been able to further improve precipitation tests by attaching microscopic latex beads to the constant end of the antibody. Since it is only the variable ends of the antibody that bind antigen, adding a bead to the constant end will not interfere with the binding of the antigen and the antibody. Let's say you have made antibody that binds an antigen on the surface of the measles virus. Viruses are so small you probably would not see the precipitation between virus particles and their antibodies; however, if you mix a patient sample that contains the measles virus with anti-measles antibodies with attached latex beads, the viruses will bind multiple antibodies, and the antibodies will bind multiple viruses. This will cause the antibodies to concentrate together, and since the latex beads are attached to the anti-bodies, these will also be drawn together.

As a result, if the antigen that reacts with the antibody is present in the patient sample (in this case, the antigens on the surface of the measles virus), the beads will form clumps that are visible. A similar method is used in the modern version of the Lancefield *Streptococcus* identification test (see box on page 112). Antibodies against the major Lancefield Group polysaccharides are modified with latex beads. If the bacterial sample you were testing were a Group B species, you would get a grainy appearance in a spot containing the anti-B serum, but not in any of the others.

FLUORESCENT ANTIBODIES

Certain chemicals have the ability to absorb energy from ultraviolet (UV) light. The energy of this light causes the chemicals to become excited, and they release energy, but with a longer wavelength than the UV light used to excite the chemicals. When the wavelength of the released energy is in the visible range, you can actually see the chemicals glow under UV light (Figure 9.2). You may have seen this demonstrated in a geology museum where certain minerals absorb UV light and give off visible light. The color of the visible light released depends on the chemical being excited. Specific chemicals will often glow a particular color because they always release light of the same wavelength.

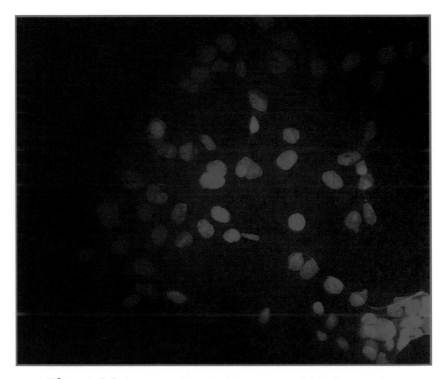

Figure 9.2 Fluorescent antibodies are powerful tools in modern medical diagnostics. Antibodies are made against a particular antigen (for instance, a particular protein or a surface antigen on a bacterial cell). The antibody is chemically modified by adding a fluorescent dye to the constant end of the antibody molecule. When the antibodies bind to the target, they concentrate around it in high numbers. This brings lots of fluorescent dye molecules to surround the target. If you illuminate the sample with UV light or a laser, the fluorescent dye will absorb the high energy light and release light in a specific, visible wavelength. This causes the dye molecules to glow and since the dye molecules surround the target, the target will appear to glow under the microscope, as can be seen here.

There are a number of chemicals commonly used to make antibodies fluorescent. Some will glow red, others green, and still others will glow different colors. These chemicals can be chemically attached to the constant region of an antibody without interfering with the ability of the chemical to fluoresce. When used with an ultraviolet microscope, fluorescent antibodies become powerful tools for diagnosis.

For example, let's say you want to develop a test for cholera. Cholera is a serious disease that results in severe diarrhea. If left untreated, a person with cholera can die within days from dehydration. The first step in creating a fluorescent antibody test for cholera would be to make a killed suspension of cholera cells. These cells could not reproduce or cause disease, but would retain the surface antigens. If you injected the killed cells into a laboratory animal, you would soon find antibodies against cholera in the serum of the animal. If you isolated this antibody and attached a fluorescent molecule that glows red under UV light to the constant region of the anti-cholera antibody, you could detect the cholera bacterium because it would glow red under a UV microscope in the presence of the fluorescent antibody.

Why does the bacterium glow? The variable end of the antibody would bind to the surface antigens on the bacterium. Since there are many of these surface antigens, you would basically surround the cell with antibodies which contain the fluorescent tags. As a result, there would be enough fluorescent chemical molecules around the cells to make the cell glow red. If, however, the patient had diarrhea from a different bacterium, the antibodies would not attach to the cells so the cells would not appear to glow under the microscope. You can see that the specific nature of antibodies makes fluorescent antibodies very powerful tools for identification of specific microorganisms. There are fluorescent antibody kits available for many of the most common disease-causing bacteria, fungi, and viruses.

ENZYME-LINKED ANTIBODY KITS

Another very powerful tool using antibodies is the enzyme-linked antibody. This is very similar to the fluorescent antibody test except an enzyme is attached to the constant region of the antibody rather than a fluorescent chemical. Remember that an enzyme is a protein that drives a particular reaction. It is a biological catalyst. One commonly used enzyme for this purpose is horseradish peroxidase. A peroxidase is an enzyme that breaks down peroxide to oxygen and water. There are also certain chemicals that have peroxide groups on them that go from a colorless compound to a colored compound when peroxidase acts upon them. By isolating peroxidase from horseradish you can chemically attach the enzyme to the constant region of an antibody. When you do, any time an antibody binds to an antigen, it will carry the enzyme with it.

A good example of an enzyme-linked antibody test is the typical home pregnancy test. When a woman becomes pregnant, she will produce certain protein hormones that are normally absent or in very low concentration. These hormones can be detected in the urine of a pregnant woman. If a woman thinks she might be pregnant, she can take a urine sample and dip the end of a test dipstick into the urine sample. If she is pregnant, the hormone will be in relatively high concentration and will stick to the dipstick. The antibody will then be added and will bind to the surface of the antigen on the dipstick. The substrate for peroxidase is also present in the mixture. If enough enzyme adheres to the dipstick because there is enough hormone present to bind the antibody, the concentration of peroxidase will be high enough to convert the enzyme substrate to a colored product. If the indicator on the test strip changes color, the chances are very high that she is pregnant. As with fluorescent antibody kits, hundreds of commercial, enzyme-linked antibody tests are available for both home and laboratory use.

MONOCLONAL ANTIBODIES

We have seen a few examples of how antibodies can be used for specific diagnostic tests. Perhaps you are wondering how we get these antibodies. The most common method for making specific antibodies is the monoclonal procedure. Monoclonal means "one clone." In other words, a monoclonal antibody only makes antibody against a single antigen.

If you inject a laboratory animal with a killed bacterial preparation, the animal's immune system will make antibodies against a large number of antigens on the surface of the bacterial cell. In addition, that animal has been exposed to countless other foreign antigens so its serum will contain many antibodies with specificity for different antigens. This serum is called a polyclonal serum because it has antibodies to lots of different antigens. It would seem impossible for you to get a serum with only one specific antibody, and when you use blood serum from an animal this is always the case. So how do you get monoclonal antibodies? To do so, you have to isolate specific B cells and find a way to keep them growing in artificial media as a cell culture. The problem is that B cells can only divide a few times before the cells die. This is true for all cells, except for cancer cells. Cancer cells are said to be immortal. They keep reproducing as long as they have nutrients. The secret to making monoclonal antibodies is to fuse together a B cell with a cancer cell. The resulting cells are a **hybridoma** (hybrid meaning made of more than once cell, "oma" meaning cancer cell).

To begin this process, you start with a laboratory animal, most commonly a mouse. The mouse is injected with the antigen you want to detect. Let us assume we will use protein X as our antigen. We take a pure preparation of protein X and inject it under the skin of the mouse. Two weeks later we repeat this process and continue to do so every two weeks for about two months. At the end of that time, we take a small sample of blood from the mouse and test to see if it has antibodies against protein X. We find that it does contain these antibodies. This tells us that the mouse is making B cells that produce antibodies that react with protein X.

After several injections of protein X, there are probably many B cells making that particular antibody because of the multiple rounds of B cell amplification. The next step is to isolate one or more of those B cells from all the others. You may remember that the spleen is one of the immune organs of the body. If we surgically remove the spleen from the mouse and break it down into individual cells, some of those will be B cells and hopefully some of the B cells will be those programmed to make anti-protein X antibodies. We next purify all the B cells

REBECCA CRAIGHILL LANCEFIELD, A WOMAN AHEAD OF HER TIME

The sciences, until the past 40 years or so, were dominated by men. Microbiology and its related sciences are a notable exception to that rule. Women have played pivotal roles in the development of microbiology. One example of an early female pioneer of microbiology and immunology is Rebecca Craighill Lancefield. Dr. Lancefield developed an interest in a genus of bacteria, *Streptococcus*, very early in her career and continued to study this group for many years. The species of bacteria in this group were frequently associated with serious diseases, including strep throat, scarlet fever, and rheumatic fever. She found that the species of this group that could cause the most serious diseases were often **hemolytic**. That means if you grew them on agar plates (a solid medium for cultivation of bacteria) that contained whole red blood cells, these bacteria would cause the blood cells to lyse, creating a clear area around the growth area for the bacterium (blood agar is normally a cloudy red agar). Unfortunately, it was very difficult to tell one hemolytic (red blood cell lysing) species from another.

Dr. Lancefield soon discovered that different species of *Streptoccocus* had different polysaccharides on their surfaces. **Polysaccharides** are large complex molecules made up of simple sugars connected together. These polysaccharides were big enough to be immunogenic. Dr. Lancefield began to purify these polysaccharides from each of her species and to use them to make antibodies. In 1933 she published a report in a scientific from all other cells in the spleen tissue. Using a few chemical tricks, we can actually fuse the B cells to cancer cells called myeloma cells. These cells can reproduce continually. The resulting cells are hybridomas, fusions of cancer cells and B cells. These hybridoma cells have the properties of continual reproduction, but contain the programmed gene for making the anti-protein X antibody.

journal that proposed and demonstrated an immunological test to distinguish different groups of *Streptococci* (plural for *Streptococcus*). She demonstrated that antibodies made against a specific polysaccharide from a species of this group could precipitate the antigens isolated from the bacteria. This could be observed visually on a microscope slide. Rebecca Lancefield developed one of the most powerful tools for diagnosis of disease for her time. The contribution Rebecca Lancefield made lives on. Her Lancefield Groups of *Streptoccoci* and her antibodies for their detection are still the definitive test for classifying pathogenic bacteria of this genus. Rebecca Lancefield continued an impressive career. She became the second woman to serve as President of the Society of American Bacteriology, which later became the American Society for Microbiology, the oldest and largest biological society in the world. In 1961, she became the only woman to serve as President of the American Association of Immunologists, and in 1970 Rebecca Lancefield was awarded one of the highest honors for science in the United States when she was elected to the membership of the National Academy of Sciences and became only the twelfth female member of the Academy.

Rebecca Lancefield left her mark on science. She was one of the first scientists to show a practical, diagnostic application for immunology. Her role as immunologist and scientist continues to inspire young women and men to enter the microbiological and immunological sciences.

Rebecca Lancefield was one of the most influential women in the history of microbiology. Her work with the serological types (different antigen types) of the genus *Streptococcus* in the 1930s developed a powerful tool for diagnosing many serious infections, including streptococcal pneumonia, strep throat, and Group B strep infections that are leading causes of deaths in newborns. The Lancefield typing system is still used today to classify species in this important genus of pathogens.

Next dilute the myeloma cells so that a small volume can be added to each of several small wells on a special tissue culture plate. Add tissue culture media to the wells and the hybridomas grow. As they do, they secrete antibodies. Some of these will be fusions from B cells that make anti-protein X antibody, but most will make other antibodies. How can we tell them apart? Allow the cells to grow for several hours. Soon the medium in the wells of the tissue culture plates will be filled with the antibodies made by that particular hydridoma.

In another tissue culture plate, we add a small amount of protein X and cause it to attach to the bottom of the well in the plate. Next, take a small amount of serum from each of the wells of your hybridomas and add each serum sample to a different well on the tissue culture plate. If the serum contains antibodies against something other than protein X, the antibodies will not bind to the protein, but if the antibodies have variable regions that bind protein X, the antibodies will stick to the protein and therefore stick to the well. Wash the wells out, and only the antibodies that specifically bind to protein X will stay in the well. All other antibodies wash away.

The next step is to determine which wells have antibodies in them. All the antibodies we are testing are mouse IgG antibodies. Remember that this is a protein and the constant region of all mouse IgG antibodies are the same, that is, they have the same antigens in them. If we purify IgG from mouse serum and inject it into another animal, a goat for example, the goat's immune system sees the mouse IgG as a foreign protein, and it makes antibodies that bind the constant region of the mouse antibody. If we then purify antibody from the goat and attach horseradish peroxidase to the constant region of the goat antibody, the variable region of the goat antibody will bind to the constant region of the mouse antibody. We take a sample of goat antibody with peroxidase attached and add it to each well in the second tissue culture plate, the one with protein X and the various fluid samples from our hybridomas. If there is mouse antibody in the well (this can only happen if the mouse antibody has bound to protein X), the goat antibody will bind the constant region of the mouse IgG molecule. Those wells with mouse IgG will bind the goat antibody, and those without it will not.

Once again we wash out the wells to remove any goat antibody that is not tightly fixed to the well through the mouse antibody and the protein X (this is called a "sandwich antibody technique" because it has different layers). Finally, we add a small amount of the peroxidase reagent to the wells. The wells with peroxide will only change color if the goat antibody is attached to the plate, which only happens if the mouse antibody is attached to protein X. This last event can only occur if the hybridoma in the well of the first tissue culture plate resulted from fusion of a B cell that makes an anti-protein X antibody. Since we know which well each serum sample came from, we can determine which hybridomas make the monoclonal antibodies we want. We can transfer these cells to larger tissue culture containers and make large amounts of antibody. We can also store some of the hybridoma cells in a very cold freezer and preserve them. In the future, when we need more antibody, we remove a frozen sample of the hybridoma, let it thaw, and transfer it to fresh tissue culture medium. The hybridoma cells will grow and secrete more of our anti-protein B antibody. With a little care, we now have an unlimited supply of this specific antibody and we can produce enough to make enzyme linked tests or fluorescent antibody tests.

CONNECTIONS

As you have moved through this book you have learned what parts of the body make up the immune system, how the immune system works to help you, and sometimes hurt you, and how we can use the power of the immune system to make very specific diagnostic tests. I hope this book has sparked an interest in the immune system for you and that some of the readers will consider a career in immunology. Immunology is one of the fastest-growing and largest market areas in the biological sciences. With all that we have learned about the immune system, there is still much more to be learned. Perhaps you will be one of the future scientists who answer some of the remaining mysteries of our body's most fascinating system, the immune system.

Glossary

Acquired Immune Deficiency Syndrome (AIDS) A deadly disease syndrome that develops after infection with the Human Immuno-deficiency Virus (HIV).

Acquired Immune System A natural defense mechanism that seems to be limited to vertebrate animals. It involves the ability to identify molecules as foreign to the body and to produce specific proteins or cells for the removal of those foreign molecules. The acquired immune system requires exposure to the foreign molecule before the body will respond.

Active Artificial Immunity A response by the body to develop antibodies or immune active cells as a consequence of an unnatural exposure to a foreign material. Development of immunity in response to a vaccine is an example of active artificial immunity.

Active Natural Immunity A response by the body to develop antibodies or immune active cells as a consequence of a natural exposure to a foreign material. An example would be development of immunity to a disease after initially acquiring that disease. This would prevent you from having the disease again in the future.

Alternate Complement Pathway A series of proteins found in the serum of the blood. These proteins initiate a cascade of reactions that are independent of antibodies. Ultimately the proteins create holes in infecting bacterial or other foreign cells that lead to cell lysis.

Anaphylactic Reaction An immune reaction, usually to a foreign antigen found in the blood that sets off a severe inflammatory response. Blood pressure drops rapidly and death can result.

Antibody A protein made by B lymphocytes that has the ability to bind to specific foreign antigens. The attachment of antibodies to a foreign material leads to its destruction by the body.

Antigen A molecule that has a particular surface structure that is bound by an antibody.

B Cell A white blood cell in the lymphoid family. These cells are central to the humoral immune system as they develop into plasma cells that produce antibodies, and memory cells that retain the ability to make antibodies if a particular antigen is experienced in the future.

B Cell Amplification A series of events controlled by lymphokines. The B cell with the ability to bind a particular antigen is stimulated to reproduce when the antigen is presented to it. During reproduction, these B cells differentiate into plasma cells and memory cells.

Basophil A white blood cell in the polymorphonucleocyte family. These cells contain granules that bind basic dyes. The granules contain histamine, heparin, and a number of other chemicals that stimulate inflammatory response.

Cell-Mediated Immunity A form of acquired immune defense where cytotoxic T cells recognize our own cells that have become compromised either by becoming cancerous or by viral infection. The cytotoxic T cells release proteins called perforins that create holes in the compromised host cells and result in cell lysis and death.

Classical Complement Pathway A series of sequential reactions of proteins found in the serum of blood. These proteins initiate the reaction by binding to foreign cells with attached antibodies. The binding of the first complement protein leads to the cleavage and binding of others, ultimately leading to lysis of the foreign cells.

Complement Proteins The collection of blood serum proteins that are involved in the complement cascade reactions.

Complement System See **complement proteins**.

Cytotoxic T Cell Antigen-specific T cells that bind to our own cells when they have become infected with viruses or have become cancerous. These cells release perforins that lead to lysis of the compromised cells.

Eosinophil Specific white blood cells of the polymorphonucleocyte family. These cells contain granules that bind acidic dyes. The granules of these cells contain powerful enzymes and chemicals that can lead to the destruction of invading foreign cells. Eosinophils are especially important in fighting fungal, protozoal, and worm infections.

Epidemic A disease that affects many individuals in a community, population, or the global community all at one time.

Epithelial Cells The class of human cells that make up the layers of the skin and mucus membranes.

Erythrocyte Red blood cells.

Hemolytic Having the ability to lyse red blood cells. This is usually due to the presence of enzymes called hemolysins or lipases.

Hemopoiesis The production of blood cells.

Human Immunodeficiency Virus (HIV) An RNA virus commonly believed to be the source of AIDS.

Glossary

Humoral Immune System The collection of cells and cell products that lead to the production of antibodies. B cells, T helper cells, and macrophages are all important contributors to the humoral immune system.

Hybridoma A cell made by fusing one cell type to a carcinoma (cancer) cell. This is used in the production of monoclonal antibodies by fusing B cells to carcinomas. Hybridomas can be grown indefinitely in tissue culture.

Immunity The ability to resist infection.

Immunogen Antigens that are sufficiently large enough to trigger the immune system to produce antibodies against one or more sites on the immunogen. All immunogens are antigens, but some antigens are too small to be immunogens.

Immunoglobulin The class of blood proteins produced by B cells that is commonly referred to as antibodies. There are five distinct classes of immunoglobulins in humans.

Inflammation A response to invasion by foreign material, or damage to cellular tissue, that results in dialysis of the blood vessels. This causes fluid to move from the blood stream to the affected site, causing the site to become hot, red, and painful.

Inflammatory Mediators Chemicals that stimulate the immune response. Some inflammatory mediators are made by our own bodies. Others are components of foreign cells, such as bacteria.

Inflammatory Response A series of non-specific reactions that result from damage to tissues or infection by foreign microorganisms. The response dilates blood vessels, causing fluid to leak from the circulatory system into the tissues surrounding the damaged/infected area. This results in swelling, reddening, warmth, and pain at the site.

Innate Immune System The series of defense mechanisms to infection that do not require previous exposure to a particular antigen to protect us.

Interleukin Proteins produced by one type of white blood cell that serve as signal molecules to communicate or stimulate other white blood cells.

Leukocyte A white blood cell.

Lymph Fluid derived from blood serum that bathes the tissues outside the circulatory system. It is important for transport of immune-active proteins and cells in the tissues and eventually flows back into the circulatory system through the lymphatic vessel network.

Lymphatic Any structures, tissues, organs, or cells that are actively involved in the immune system.

Lymphatic Tissue Clusters of tissue that play important roles in immune response. These tissues are less differentiated than organs, but exist as a complex of cells unlike B and T cells. Tonsils, adenoids, and Peyer's patches are all examples of lymphoid tissue.

Lymphoid Family The group of white blood cells that contains the B cells and T cells or those cells directly involved in the acquired immune response.

Lysozyme An enzyme produced in human tears that breaks down the structural molecule of bacterial cell walls.

Major Histocompatibility Complex (MHC) Proteins found on the surface of all cells in an organism. These proteins are important in defining "self-recognition" and play a critical rose in normal immune function and in organ transplant rejection. MHC I is a protein found on all cells of the body and is important in antigen presentation during cell-mediated immune response when our cells become infected or cancerous. MHC II is present almost exclusively on phagocytic cells and is essential in presentation of foreign antigens to activate the humoral (antibody-based) immune system.

M.A.L.T.—Mucosal Associated Lymphoid Tissue Patches of tissue found just below the mucous membranes and that are important sites for production of secreted antibodies.

Macrophage Large white blood cells that develop when neutrophils leave the circulatory system and enter the surrounding tissues. These are phagocytic cells that ingest and break down foreign microorganisms and other foreign antigens.

Memory Cell A lymphoid cell derived from a B cell upon first activation. These cells are stored in the body and have the ability to be stimulated to replicate and to make new plasma cells upon subsequent exposure to a foreign antigen.

Microorganism Any of a group of single celled living organisms too small to see without magnification. Major groups include the bacteria, the fungi, the protozoa, the algae, and the non-living group of agents called viruses.

Glossary

Monocyte The most common form of agranualar white blood cell. Monocytes contain a single nuclear domain.

Mononuclear Leukocyte See **monocyte**.

Mucus A thick, sticky polymer that coats the mucous membranes, entrapping foreign material such as dust, bacteria, and fungi, therefore preventing them from penetrating into deeper tissues.

Mucous Membranes The membranes that line the respiratory, digestive, and reproductive tracts, as well as the sockets of the eyes.

Natural Killer Cells Non-B, Non-C cells that lyse target human cells by the production of perforins.

Neutrophil The predominant form of white blood cell. Neutrophils stain poorly and contain powerful enzymes that destroy foreign materials.

Non-specific Reactive Responses These are immune responses that do not require a specific antigen for initiation.

Null Lymphocytes Lymphocytes that have not differentiated between B or T cells.

Passive Artificial Immunity A form of borrowed immunity where one obtains antibodies made from another person. The most common example is receipt of immunoglobulin injections to ward off infection.

Passive Barrier Defenses Physical structures that exclude foreign materials from entering the protected regions of the body. These include the skin and mucous membranes.

Passive Natural Immunity A form of borrowed immunity where one obtains antibodies made from another person. The most common example is IgG molecules that cross the placenta from the mother to protect a baby or the ingestion of antibodies from a mother's breast milk.

Perforin Proteins produced by cells that lead to formation of holes in damaged human cells.

Peyer's Patches (G.A.L.T.) Patches of lymphoid tissue found below the lining of the lower digestive track. These play an important role in protecting the body by secreting antibodies into the intestine.

Phagocytic Cells White blood cells with the ability to bind and engulf foreign materials.

Phagocytosis The act of engulfing a solid, foreign object by a cell.

Plasma Cell A cell type that is produced when B cells are activated. Plasma cells become dedicated factories for the production of antibody molecules.

Polymorphonuclear Leukocyte Granular white blood cells that have multiple staining regions.

Polysaccharide A polymer made of repeating simple sugars.

S.A.L.T. —Skin Associated Lymphoid Tissue Tissues that serve as sites for activation of B or T cells and that promote the secretion of antibodies (IgA) across the skin.

T Cell A lymphoid white blood cell that matures in the thymus. The three major classes of T cells are helper T cells, cyototoxic T cells, and suppressor T cells.

T Helper Cell One of three major classes of T lymphocytes (T cells). These cells are responsible for stimulation of both humoral (antibody-based) and cell-mediated immune responses and are the target of the HIV virus that causes AIDS.

T Suppressor Cell A lymphoid white blood cell that helps to suppress immune response and that is probably involved in selecting against B cells or T cells that would attack normal host cells.

Tear Duct An opening in the corner of the eye where tears are released.

Vaccination The process of intentionally exposing a person to a foreign antigen with the hope that the resulting response will be protection from that pathogen in the future.

Vaccine Any material used to vaccinate. Common vaccines are live attenuated vaccines, killed cell vaccines, and vaccination with specific foreign antigens.

White Blood Cell The family of blood cells that is essential to immune response.

Bibliography

Abbas, Abul, Andrew H. Lichtman, and Jordan S. Prober. *Cellular and Molecular Immunology.* 4th ed. Philadelphia: W. H. Saunders Company. 2000.

Alcamo, I. Edward. *AIDS: The Biological Basis.* 2nd ed. Dubuque, Iowa: William C. Brown Publishers. 1997.

Atlas, Ronald. *Many Faces–Many Microbes: Personal Reflections in Microbiology.* Washington, D.C.: ASM Press. 2000.

Balkwill, Frances R. and Mic Rolph (Illustrator). *Cell Wars.* Minneapolis, Minn.: Lerner Publishing Group. 1994.

Coleman, Robert M., Mary F. Lombard, and Raymond Sicard. *Fundamental Immunology.* 2nd ed. Dubuque, Iowa: William C. Brown Publishers. 1992.

Edelson, Edward. *The Immune System.* Broomall, Pa.: Chelsea House Publishers. 2000.

Freidlander, Mark P., and Terry M. Phillips. T*he Immune System: Your Body's Disease-Fighting Army.* Minneapolis, Minn.: Lerner Publishing Group. 1998.

Goldsby, David A., Janis Rhuby, Thomas J. Kindt, and Barbara A. Osborne. *Immunology.* 4th ed. New York: W. H. Freeman and Company. 2000.

Gonzales, Doreen. *AIDS: Ten Stories of Courage.* Berkeley Heights, N.J.: Enslow Publishers. 1996.

Hyde, Margaret O., and Elizabeth Held Forsyth. *Vaccinations: From Smallpox to Cancer.* New York: Scholastic Library Publishing. 2000.

Ingraham, John L., and Catherine A. Ingraham. *Introduction to Microbiology.* 2nd ed. Pacific Grove, Calif.: Brooks Cole Publishing. 2000.

Jussim, Daniel. *AIDS and HIV: Risky Business.* Berkeley Heights, N.J.: Enslow Publishers, Inc. 1997.

Kaufmann, Stefan H., Alan Sher, and Rafi Ahmed. *Immunology of Infectious Disease.* Washington, D.C.: ASM Press. 2002.

Latta, Sara L. *Allergies.* Berkeley Heights, N.J.: Enslow Publishers, Inc. 1998.

Mims, C. A., D. Wakelin, R. Williams, I Roitt, and J. Playfair. *Medical Microbiology.* 2nd ed. Saint Louis, Mo.: Mosby Year Book, Inc. 1998.

Preston, Richard. *The Demon in the Freezer: A True Story.* New York: Random House, Inc. 2002.

Roitt, Ivan, Jonathan Brostoff, and David Male. *Immunology.* 6th ed. Saint Louis, Mo.: Mosby Year Book, Inc. 2001.

Shilts, Randy. *And the Band Played On: Politics, People, and the AIDS Epidemic.* New York: Saint Martin's Press. 1999.

Sompayrac, Lauren. *How the Immune System Works.* 2nd ed. Oxford, UK: Blackwell Press. 2002.

Further Reading

Preston, Richard. *The Demon in the Freezer: A True Story*. New York: Random House, Inc. 2002.

Hyde, Margaret O. and Elizabeth Held Forsyth. *Vaccinations: From Smallpox to Cancer*. New York: Scholastic Library Publishing. 2000.

Edelson, Edward. *The Immune System*. Broomall, Pa.: Chelsea House Publishers. 2000.

Latta, Sara L. *Allergies*. Berkeley Heights, N.J.: Enslow Publishers, Inc. 1998.

Gonzales, Doreen. *AIDS: Ten Stories of Courage*. Berkeley Heights, N.J.: Enslow Publishers, Inc. 1996.

Jussim, Daniel. *AIDS and HIV: Risky Business*. Berkeley Heights, N.J.: Enslow Publishers, Inc. 1997.

Freidlander, Mark P. and Terry M. Phillips. *The Immune System: Your Body's Disease-Fighting Army*. Minneapolis: Lerner Publishing Group. 1998.

Balkwill, Frances, and Mic Rolph (Illustrator). *Cell Wars*. Minneapolis: Lerner Publishing Group. 1994.

Websites

www.cehs.siu.edu/ffix/medmicro/igs/htm
An explanation of how immunizations work

www.ecbt.org/howdoim.htm
Lymphocytes and antibody production

www.cellsalive.com/antibody.htm
Interactive description of B and T cell activation

www.microbelibrary.org/images/suchman/htmlpages/immune_gif.html
Interactive summary of phagocytosis

www.microbelibrary.org/images/tterry/anim/phago053.html
Video of the classical complement pathway

www.microbelibrary.org/images/barnum/images/barnumtit(qt2s).mov

Unit (metric)		Metric to English	English to Metric	
LENGTH				
Kilometer	km	1 km 0.62 mile (mi)	1 mile (mi)	1.609 km
Meter	m	1 m 3.28 feet (ft)	1 foot (ft)	0.305 m
Centimeter	cm	1 cm 0.394 inches (in)	1 inch (in)	2.54 cm
Millimeter	mm	1 mm 0.039 inches (in)	1 inch (in)	25.4 mm
Micrometer	μm			
WEIGHT (MASS)				
Kilogram	kg	1 kg 2.2 pounds (lbs)	1 pound (lbs)	0.454 kg
Gram	g	1 g 0.035 ounces (oz)	1 ounce (oz)	28.35 g
Milligram	mg			
Microgram	μg			
VOLUME				
Liter	L	1 L 1.06 quarts	1 gallon (gal)	3.785 L
			1 quart (qt)	0.94 L
			1 pint (pt)	0.47 L
Milliliter	mL or cc	1 mL 0.034 fluid ounce (fl oz)	1 fluid ounce (fl oz)	29.57 mL
Microliter	μL			
TEMPERATURE				
$°C = 5/9 \ (°F - 32)$		$°F = 9/5 \ (°C + 32)$		

Index

Index

page:

13: Courtesy World Health Organization (WHO)
15: © SIU/Visuals Unlimited
19: © Lester V. Bergman/CORBIS
23: © Jim Zuckerman/CORBIS
28: Lambda Science Artwork
31: © Noelle Nardone
33: Lambda Science Artwork
37: Lambda Science Artwork
39: © David Phillips/Visuals Unlimited
44: © Lester V. Bergman/CORBIS
46: Lambda Science Artwork
50: Lambda Science Artwork
52: Lambda Science Artwork
59: Lambda Science Artwork

64: © Noelle Nardone
72: Lambda Science Artwork
74: ©William J. Johnson/Visuals Unlimited
80: © Bettmann/CORBIS
83: Courtesy CDC, Public Health Image Library (PHIL)
89: Lambda Science Artwork
91: © SIU/Visuals Unlimited
94: © SIU/Visuals Unlimited
95: © Ken Greer/Visuals Unlimited
98: Lambda Science Artwork
99: © Sid Bloom
105: Lambda Science Artwork
105: © Beth Reger
114: © Rockefeller University Archives

Coca-Cola, Sprite, Diet Coke, Fanta, and Beverly are registered trademarks of the Coca-Cola Company.

About the Author

Dr. Gregory J. Stewart completed his Ph.D. in microbiology from the University of California at Davis. His post-doctoral training was conducted at Exxon Research and Engineering, and and E. I. DuPont de Nemours and Company. He spent seven years at the University of South Florida as an Assistant and Associate Professor of Biology. In 1993 he joined the Biology Department of the State University of West Georgia (then West Georgia College) where he served as Department Chair for eight years. After one year as Assistant Dean of Arts and Sciences at West Georgia, Dr. Stewart accepted a senior fellowship with the Bureau of Arms Control at the United States Department of State where he is currently employed. His duties at the State Department include coordination of the Biological and Toxins Weapons Convention (Treaty) and as advisor to all bureaus and other federal agencies on issues related to microbiology, biological weapons reduction, bioterrorism/counter-terrorism threat reduction and response, and non-proliferation of weapons of mass destruction. He also serves on the National Institute of Allergy and Infectious Disease Biodefense vaccine development review panel and on the Small Business and Innovative Research panel for biodefense response, as well as serving as ad hoc reviewer for several other funding agencies and professional journals. He is the author of more than 30 scientific publications. Dr. Stewart is married to Patricia, is the step-father of three children, and the grandfather of one.